Empowering the Giving of Your Church

PASTOR FRANK DAMAZIO

Luke 6:38

IF YOU GIVE, YOU WILL RECEIVE. YOUR GIFT WILL RETURN TO YOU IN FULL MEASURE, PRESSED DOWN, SHAKEN TOGETHER TO MAKE ROOM FOR MORE, AND RUNNING OVER. WHATEVER MEASURE YOU USE IN GIVING--LARGE OR SMALL--IT WILL BE USED TO MEASURE WHAT IS GIVEN BACK TO YOU.
[THE NEW LIVING TRANSLATION]

Published by City Christian Publishing
9200 NE Fremont
Portland, Oregon 97220

Printed in U.S.A.

City Christian Publishing is a ministry of City Bible Church, and is dedicated to serving the local church and its leaders through the production and distribution of quality materials. It is our prayer that these materials, proven in the context of the local church, will equip leaders in exalting the Lord and extending His kingdom.

For a free catalog of additional resources from City Christian Publishing, please call 1-800-777-6057.

Empowering the Giving Of Your Church – Student Handbook
ISBN 1-59383-012-2
© Copyright 2003 by City Christian Publishing
All Rights Reserved

All scripture quotations, unless otherwise indicated, are taken from the Holy Bible, New King James Version. Copyright © 1982, Thomas Nelson, Inc. Used by permission. All rights reserved.

All rights reserved, including the right to reproduce this book, or any portions thereof, in any form. No part of this book may be reproduced or transmitted in any form or by any means, electronic or mechanical, mechanical, magnetic, chemical, optical, manual, or otherwise, including photocopying, recording, or by any information storage or retrieval system without written permission from City Bible Publishing. All rights for publishing this book or portions thereof in other languages are contracted by the author.

Every effort has been made to supply complete and accurate information. However, neither the publisher nor the author assume any responsibility for its use, nor for any infringements of patents or other rights of third parties that would result.

All Rights Reserved
Printed in the United States of America

Empowering the Giving of Your Church

Table of Contents

Seminar Notes

Empowering the Leader to Build a Giving Church 9

Empowering the Nine Keys for Giving 17

Empowering the Giving of Tithes and Offerings 37

Empowering and Releasing the Business Person 57

Empowering People for Supernatural Provision 65

Sermon Notes

Giving, Receiving and Prospering 71

Call to Faith Harvest Giving 79

Biblical Money Management 87

We Can Touch The World 93

Call to Great Faith 103

Great Vision Takes the Challenge 115

# Empowering the Giving of Your Church

Empowering the Giving of Your Church

Eight-Fold Purpose of This Seminar

Encourage — and equip leaders to teach, preach and plan for financial blessings and financial abundance

Educate — the leader and remove any faulty theology concerning finances, giving, receiving, prospering and any faulty theology about the nature and attributes of God

Enlighten — the leader by giving practical and spiritual principles that can be applied in any local church setting with proven biblical results

Empower — the leader toward a great faith that will believe for and pray for the supernatural release of abundant resources

Enlarge — the leader by removing any limitations toward finances in the mind, heart and spirit of all leaders, thus freeing them to fulfill their mission with divine supernatural provisions

Energize — by providing preaching and teaching materials which will assist the leader in the establishing of financial strategies and resources

Enliven — the leader through stories, testimonies, insights, principles and practical suggestions about empowering the giving of local congregations

Engrave — onto the leader's mind, heart and spirit the word of God that lays a sure foundation for blessing, honor, prosperity and longevity in the work of God

# Empowering the Giving of Your Church

Empowering the Giving of Your Church

Scriptures That Empower the Giving Spirit

PSALM 112:1
Praise the Lord! Blessed is the man who fears the Lord, who delights greatly in His commandments.

PROVERBS 3:5-6
Trust in the Lord with all your heart, and lean not on your own understanding; in all your ways acknowledge Him, and He shall direct your paths.

MICAH 6:8
He has shown you, O man, what is good; And what does the Lord require of you but to do justly, to love mercy, and to walk humbly with your God?

PROVERBS 11:24
There is one who scatters, yet increases more; and there is one who withholds more than is right, but it leads to poverty.

PROVERBS 19:17 He who has pity on the poor lends to the Lord, and He will pay back what he has given.

1 CORINTHIANS 4:1-2
Let a man so consider us, as servants of Christ and stewards of the mysteries of God. Moreover it is required in stewards that one be found faithful.

1 TIMOTHY 6:18-19
Let them do good, that they be rich in good works, ready to give, willing to share, storing up for themselves a good foundation for the time to come, that they may lay hold on eternal life.

LUKE 6:38
Give, and it will be given to you: good measure, pressed down, shaken together, and running over will be put into your bosom. For with the same measure that you use, it will be measured back to you.

MATTHEW 25:21
"His lord said to him, 'Well done, good and faithful servant; you were faithful over a few things, I will make you ruler over many things. Enter into the joy of your lord.'"

MATTHEW 6:19-21
"Do not lay up for yourselves treasures on earth, where moth and rust destroy and where thieves break in and steal; but lay up for yourselves treasures in heaven, where neither moth nor rust destroys and where thieves do not break in and steal. For where your treasure is, there your heart will be also."

MATTHEW 6:24
"No one can serve two masters; for either he will hate the one and love the other, or else he will be loyal to the one and despise the other. You cannot serve God and mammon."

JOSHUA 24:15
Choose for yourselves this day whom you will serve, whether the gods which your fathers served that were on the other side of the River, or the gods of the Amorites, in whose land you dwell. But as for me and my house, we will serve the Lord.

Empowering the Giving of Your Church

MATTHEW 6:33
But seek first the kingdom of God and His righteousness, and all these things shall be added to you.

PSALM 119:72
The law of Your mouth is better to me than thousands of coins of gold and silver.

PROVERBS 16:2
All the ways of a man are pure in his own eyes, but the Lord weighs the spirits.

NUMBERS 30:2
If a man vows a vow to the Lord, or swears an oath to bind himself by some agreement, he shall not break his word; he shall do according to all that proceeds out of his mouth.

DEUTERONOMY 23:21
When you make a vow to the Lord your God, you shall not delay to pay it; for the Lord your God will surely require it of you, and it would be sin to you.

DEUTERONOMY 23:23
That which has gone from your lips you shall keep and perform, for you voluntarily vowed to the Lord your God what you have promised with your mouth.

ECCLESIASTES 5:4-5
When you make a vow to God, do not delay to pay it; for He has no pleasure in fools. Pay what you have vowed—better not to vow than to vow and not pay.

ACTS 5:29
But Peter and the other apostles answered and said: "We ought to obey God rather than men."

PROVERBS 16:9
A man's heart plans his way, but the Lord directs his steps.

LUKE 8:18
Therefore take heed how you hear. For whoever has, to him more will be given; and whoever does not have, even what he seems to have will be taken from him.

PHILIPPIANS 2:3
Let nothing be done through selfish ambition or conceit, but in lowliness of mind let each esteem others better than himself.

PROVERBS 28:27
He who gives to the poor will not lack, but he who hides his eyes will have many curses.

MATTHEW 23:12
And whoever exalts himself will be humbled, and he who humbles himself will be exalted.

PROVERBS 29:23
A man's pride will bring him low, but the humble in spirit will retain honor.

ISAIAH 66:2
"For all those things My hand has made, and all those things exist," says the Lord. "But on this one will I look: On him who is poor and of a contrite spirit, and who trembles at My word."

MATTHEW 13:52
Then He said to them, "Therefore every scribe instructed concerning the kingdom of heaven is like a householder who brings out of his treasure things new and old."

PROVERBS 27:23-24
Be diligent to know the state of your flocks, and attend to your herds; for riches are not forever, nor does a crown endure to all generations.

Empowering the Giving of Your Church

1 Chronicles 22:14
Indeed I have taken much trouble to prepare for the house of the Lord one hundred thousand talents of gold and one million talents of silver, and bronze and iron beyond measure, for it is so abundant. I have prepared timber and stone also, and you may add to them.

Mark 12:42-44
Then one poor widow came and threw in two mites, which make a quadrans. So He called His disciples to Himself and said to them, "Assuredly, I say to you that this poor widow has put in more than all those who have given to the treasury; for they all put in out of their abundance, but she out of her poverty put in all that she had, her whole livelihood."

Proverbs 30:25
The ants are a people not strong, yet they prepare their food in the summer;

2 Corinthians 9:6
But this I say: He who sows sparingly will also reap sparingly, and he who sows bountifully will also reap bountifully.

1 Kings 10:10
Then she gave the king one hundred and twenty talents of gold, spices in great quantity, and precious stones. There never again came such abundance of spices as the queen of Sheba gave to King Solomon.

2 Kings 25:30
And as for his provisions, there was a regular ration given him by the king, a portion for each day, all the days of his life.

Luke 11:13
If you then, being evil, know how to give good gifts to your children, how much more will your heavenly Father give the Holy Spirit to those who ask Him!

Matthew 6:3-4
But when you do a charitable deed, do not let your left hand know what your right hand is doing, that your charitable deed may be in secret; and your Father who sees in secret will Himself reward you openly.

1 Timothy 6:18
Let them do good, that they be rich in good works, ready to give, willing to share.

Hebrews 13:16
But do not forget to do good and to share, for with such sacrifices God is well pleased.

Leviticus 19:10
And you shall not glean your vineyard, nor shall you gather every grape of your vineyard; you shall leave them for the poor and the stranger: I am the Lord your God.

Job 20:10
His children will seek the favor of the poor and his hands will restore his wealth.

Job 29:12
Because I delivered the poor who cried out, the fatherless and he who had no helper.

Proverbs 14:21
He who despises his neighbor sins; but he who has mercy on the poor, happy is he.

Proverbs 19:17
He who has pity on the poor lends to the Lord, and He will pay back what he has given.

Luke 12:33
Sell what you have and give alms; provide yourselves money bags which do not grow old, a treasure in the heavens that does not fail, where no thief approaches nor moth destroys.

Empowering the Giving of Your Church

Empowering Leaders to Build Giving Churches

Session 1

> The key to any success in the local church is first the leader. If the leader is empowered concerning the doctrine of giving and has great spiritual passions to see the church blessed and prospering, empowering the church will be easy. If the leader struggles with the giving doctrine and has no faith to teach or preach this doctrine, then the church will suffer.

Empowering Leaders to Build Giving Churches

I. Basic Presuppositions

A. Leaders of churches and ministries desire more financial resources to accomplish mission than what they have

B. Leaders of churches and ministries struggle to find and receive enough resources to accomplish desired mission and eventually settle for less.

C. Leaders of churches and ministries may have no clear plan in place to find sufficient resources or to increase their resources annually.

D. Leaders of churches and ministries may not see that preaching, teaching, praying, and planning for desired resources are all equally important.

E. Leaders of churches may feel they are not responsible for the increased flow of finances for the vision and ministries of the church.

> "Two things are true of congregations: congregations never have enough money and congregations have all the money they really need for God's mission."
> KENNON CALLAHAN

II. Basic Leadership Challenges

A. **Perspective Challenge**
We must see our financial challenges as spiritual, not financial. It is not about raising money. It is about developing disciples. Financial growth is not automatic. Just because people attend church does not mean they will automatically give.

B. **Reaction Challenge**
Reacting to an extreme prosperity faith message or reacting to an extreme poverty mentality are both equally destructive. Reacting to criticism about your vision stretching mentality that necessitates finances is a wrong reaction. People give more generously in an environment of positive reinforcement, encouragement and a forward-moving attitude.

> "Most pastors, church staff and lay leaders are both inadequately trained and emotionally unprepared for communicating about and actually raising the kind of money required to lead a church toward fulfillment of its vision."
> GEORGE BARNA

Empowering Leaders to Build Giving Churches

"The way to avoid mistakes is to do nothing."

"There is a need for a conversion of the heart, the mind and the purse in the Christian life."
MARTIN LUTHER

"The biggest surprise was how little stewardship education is really going on in churches today."
J. DAVID SCHMIDT

C. **Discouragement Challenge**

Financial woes are the order of the day for both the small congregations and the larger congregations. Churches are scaling back staff and programs and putting expansion programs on hold. This may cause discouragement. This may cause leaders to carry an attitude of "something is wrong with our church." A stealth crisis is looming in the future—the supply and distribution of money to support mission and ministry in the 21st century.

D. **Faith Challenge**

People do not respond to leaders who are complaining, lamenting, scolding or whining about the lack of resources. People do respond to a faith-filled leader who is growing, developing and advancing the vision with great expectation for financial blessing and provisions. People live up to positively communicated expectancies, but people live down to negatively communicated expectancies.

E. **Strategy Challenge**

"Few leaders are addressing the issue. It is an issue that affects every congregation, regardless of size or location, and every institution supported by organized religion." (Leadership Network) The leader must have a strategy that involves the word, preaching, prayer and communication into every level of the church. Youth, young adults, young marrieds, single parents, senior citizens—all the church must be touched with strategy.

F. **Preaching Challenge**

Goetz reported that most pastors tithe but they don't consistently teach, preach or encourage the church to tithe. (Leadership Journal) We are not to be preoccupied with money. We are not to lose our true focus of preaching a balanced and whole Bible. We lose our ministry integrity when we take a narrow focus on money issues only. A Christian Stewardship Association survey revealed that 85% of pastors feel they have not been taught or empowered to teach principles of biblical stewardship and finance.

G. **People Challenge**

Recent research shows a 26-year decline in giving percentages among evangelicals. Giving has shrunk 1.5% to 3.5% with only one or two out of 10 Christians giving 10% of their income to the Lord's work. Money is a sensitive issue with people. "What right does the church have to concern itself with my money?" Statistics can be revealing, but we have the power in and through the Holy Spirit to break the predictions of statistics. We can believe and teach for disciples, not just for church attendees.

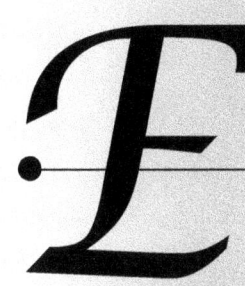

Empowering Leaders to Build Giving Churches

III. The Vision and Resource Factor

> "A great leader takes people where they don't really want to go, but ought to go."
> ROSALYN CARTER

A. The Essentials for Effective Vision

1. The people are committed and equipped to function in fulfilling this vision.

2. The people are divinely energized and unified together to accomplish God-given vision.

3. The leadership controls hindering tendencies that would stagnate and divide vision.

4. The leadership is strong, focused and committed to the prophetic vision which has been agreed upon. Every effort is marshaled strategically to accomplish vision.

> "The only person who likes change is a wet baby."
> MARK TWAIN

5. Clear vision provides the church with clear direction and enables the church to move together in unity and is a motivating factor.

6. Intentional vision is a church that discerns and declares the biblical purpose of God and discerns specifically its own particular prophetic purpose and uniqueness and is willing to pay the price to fulfill it.

7. Intentional vision discerns its primary grace factor, its gifting, the strengths and the weaknesses of the congregation and the determination to release all of the resources necessary to accomplishing vision.

> "The skipper who says he has never run aground is the skipper whose boat has never left the dock."

B. The Ten Vision Realities

1. Vision always <u>demands change</u>.
   (Psalm 15:4; Psalm 55:19)

2. Vision always <u>requires faith</u>.
   (Hebrews 11:1; 1 Samuel 14:6; Deuteronomy 33:20; Habakkuk 2:4; 2 Corinthians 5:7)

Empowering Leaders to Build Giving Churches

3. Vision always <u>requires work</u>.
   (Nehemiah 4:6; Genesis 2:2; Exodus 39:32; 1 Kings 5:16; 7:14,22,29)

4. Vision usually makes <u>some people uncomfortable</u>.
   (Ezra 5:8; Ezra 4:20-24)

5. Vision is usually not <u>embraced by everyone at the same time</u>.
   (Judges 7:3; Ezra 5:5; Nehemiah 2:12-16)

6. Vision usually <u>unfolds progressively</u>.
   (Isaiah 28:13)

7. Vision usually drives everyone <u>to a new level of prayer</u>.
   (2 Corinthians 10:3-4; Nehemiah 4:7)

8. Vision provokes the enemy to attack <u>before the vision can become reality</u>.
   (Exodus 14:16; Genesis 3:15; Acts 18:10; Nehemiah 2:19-20)

9. Vision is fulfilled by a <u>visionary leadership</u> who have the heart and unity of a <u>visionary people</u>.
   (1 Corinthians 1:10; Nehemiah 4:13)

10. Vision involves the <u>sacrificial giving of our resources</u> and the <u>supernatural provision of God</u>.
    (Exodus 35:29; 36:6-7; 1 Chronicles 29:3)

> "People give to a great vision, a winning course, a God-exalting mission. People will go forward with generosity of spirit when they see the vision."

> "One of the clear challenges facing churches and faith communities today is how to transform people into faithful, committed givers that are biblically rooted."
> GEORGE GALLUP

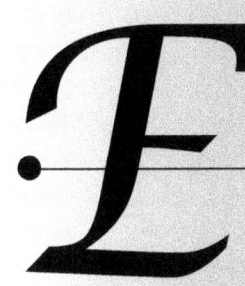

Empowering Leaders to Build Giving Churches

IV. Cultivating the Heart of a Giving Church

> "God has given us two hands. One to receive with and the other to give with. We are not cisterns made for hoarding. We are channels made for sharing."
> BILLY GRAHAM

A. Cultivating the Giving Person Strategically

1. The commitment factor must be secured.

   The goal of our ministry to every member is to help them to become a person who is born-again, water-baptized and filled with the Spirit, who is faithful to the corporate church gatherings, cell ministry and School of Equipping; joyfully gives their tithe and offerings, enjoys prayer, the Word, and worship, has a heart for winning our city to Christ and a vision for world missions, upholds family values and loves God with all their heart, soul, mind and strength. (City Bible Church Members Profile)

2. The giving person is a regular attender at church.
   a. "National Contextual Factors Influencing Church Trends" says, "Regularity of church attendance remains the number one predictor of an individual's contributions to the church."
   b. If attendance is the number one factor, then our first step in building a giving church is building a dynamic church with a strong membership and an awesome corporate church service that people are drawn into.

> "The most important aspect of tithing and stewardship is not the raising of money for the church, but the development of devoted Christians."
> FRED WOOD

B. Eight Reasons Why People Give[1]

1. Passion: They give because they believe in the cause

2. Affiliation: They give because they belong to the group

3. Tradition: They give because they have a history and practice of giving

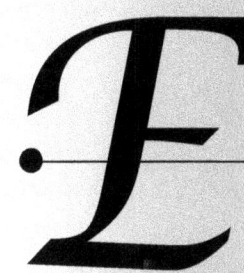

Empowering Leaders to Build Giving Churches

> "There never was a person who did anything worth doing who did not receive more than he gave."
> HENRY WARD BEECHER

4. Recognition: They give because they want to be known

5. Inspiration: They give because they are captured by the project or the presenter

6. Obligation: They give because they want to make a difference

7. Invitation: They give because they are invited or asked to give

8. Completion: They give because they are fulfilling commitment

C. Shift in percentage of givers among age-groups

Ages 18 to 32:   *31% contribute*
Ages 33 to 51:   *43% contribute*
Ages 52 to 69:   *54% contribute*
Ages 70 and above: *61% contribute*

D. Cultivating the Giving Heart
Giving starts with the Holy Spirit stirring the heart. Then a thought moves to the mind and then reaches out with an open hand to give. The giving starts with an impulse to do something beyond ourselves, an urge to share. Our spirit and heart are activated through information, scriptures, testimonies and the presence of God.

> "The only safe rule is to give more than we can spare."
> C.S. LEWIS

1. <u>Willing</u> Heart
(Exodus 25:2; 35:5,21-22)

2. <u>Stirred</u> Heart
(Exodus 35:21)

3. <u>Sacrificial</u> Heart
(Exodus 35:29)

4. <u>Loyal</u> Heart
(I Chronicles 29:3)

5. <u>Rejoicing</u> Heart
(I Chronicles 29:9)

6. <u>Wounded</u> Heart
(Luke 15:24)

---

[1] Dave Sutherland, president of Injoy Stewardship Services

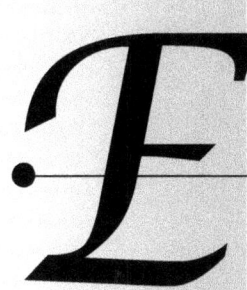

EMPOWERING NINE PROVEN GIVING KEYS

SESSION #2

> Giving to churches and church causes is generally declining nationwide. Some of the monies that, in times past, was easy for the church to receive is now going to causes the church formerly had as a church ministry. Para-church ministries are making direct appeals to churches and to individual church people and getting strong dollar support. Colleges, universities and other social services are going after the same Christian person for dollars. We also have missionary agencies and individual missionaries raising money from the church person. Then of course, there is Christian radio and television also raising funds. The church must have a very clear vision, a deep-rooted set of values and a strategy for building a giving spirit into the church.

Empowering Nine Proven Giving Keys

Keys to Unlock God's Supernatural Resources for Your Church

PERSPECTIVE	Establishing a right biblical perspective on God as a great giver who is liberal with his abundant resources and a belief in the promises in scripture concerning finances and resources. *(Psalm 84:11; 65:11; 34:8-14; John 3:16; Romans 8:32; 1 Tim 6:17; Heb 11:6)*
STEWARDSHIP	The careful and responsible management of that which God has entrusted to our care: our time, strength, talents and money. *(Luke 16:10; Matthew 25:21)*
WORKING	Working with diligence and integrity is biblical; God promises to reward hard work and the scripture connects work with success and financial blessings. *(Colossians 3:23-24; Ephesians 6:5-8; 1 Timothy 6:1-3; 2 Thess 3:6-15; Proverbs 22:29; 13:11)*
GIVING	Giving tithes and offerings activates divine law that releases the blessings of God in our personal world and supplies resources for the church to accomplish mission. *(Prov 3:9-10; 11:24; 19:17; Luke 6:38; Romans 12:6-7; Mal 3:8-10; 2 Cor 9:7; Acts 20:27,35; 1 Cor 16:1-2)*
RECEIVING	God responds to our giving by opening up opportunities to receive divine provisions both directly and indirectly from His hand. *(Malachi 3:9-10; Deut 28:8; Prov 10:22; Acts 3:5; Matt 7:8; Romans 4:21; Isaiah 40:8; Mark 10:30)*
MANAGING	God expects and requires believers to biblically manage their life, including their money and for church leaders to properly and wisely manage church resources. *(2 Timothy 1:7; Proverbs 16:32; Joshua 1:8; Psalm 1:1-3; Luke 16:1-13; Matthew 25:14-30)*
RELEASING	God desires the local church leadership to cultivate a biblical vision for those called to the marketplace, releasing the business person to use their gift of faith, giving and leadership to accomplish God's purposes. *(Psalm 8:6; 2 Corinthians 5:19; Mark 16:15; John 17:11; Proverbs 10:22; 24:25)*
PROSPERING	God desires that we receive abundantly and have more than enough so as to become a liberal giver and to see God's work have abundant resources. *(1 Chr 4:10; Pr 3:6; 22:4; Dt 28:13; Ps 118:25; 3 Jn 2; Neh 1:11; 2:20; Gen 39:2,23; Josh 1:8; 2 Chr 26:5)*
BEQUEATHING	God desires that we live wisely and leave an inheritance to continue God's work into and through the next generation. *(Job 42:15; Psalm 16:6; Proverbs 13:22; 19:14; Ezek 46:16-17)*

Empowering Nine Proven Giving Keys

#1 The Perspective Key

Perspective Definition

A way of regarding situations or topics. The capacity to view things in their true relations or relative importance. The word "perspective" used to mean a telescope or glass through which items were viewed. Viewpoint, outlook, point of view, perception.

Scriptural Perspective on God

GOD WILL BLESS YOUR WORK.
Deut 28:12 The Lord will open to you His good treasure, the heavens, to give the rain to your land in its season, and to bless all the work of your hand. You shall lend to many nations, but you shall not borrow.

GOD WILL MAKE YOUR WORK INCREASE AND PROSPER.
Deut 30:9 The Lord your God will make you abound in all the work of your hand, in the fruit of your body, in the increase of your livestock, and in the produce of your land for good. For the Lord will again rejoice over you for good as He rejoiced over your fathers,

GOD WILL KEEP HIS PROMISES TO YOU.
Josh 21:45 Not a word failed of any good thing which the Lord had spoken to the house of Israel. All came to pass.

THE LORD'S MERCY ENDURES FOREVER.
Ezra 3:11 And they sang responsively, praising and giving thanks to the Lord; "For He is good, for His mercy endures forever toward Israel." Then all the people shouted with a great shout, when they praised the Lord, because the foundation of the house of the Lord was laid.

THE GOOD HAND OF THE LORD IS UPON YOU.
Neh 2:8 ..."And a letter to Asaph the keeper of the king's forest, that he must give me timber to make beams for the gates of the citadel which pertains to the temple, for the city wall, and for the house that I will occupy." And the king granted them to me according to the good hand of my God upon me.

GOD IS GOOD AND UPRIGHT.
Ps 25:8 Good and upright is the Lord; therefore He teaches sinners in the way.

GOD IS GOOD.
Ps 34:8 Oh, taste and see that the Lord is good; blessed is the man who trusts in Him!

GOD SHOWS YOU HIS LOVINGKINDNESS.
Ps 69:16 Hear me, O Lord, for Your lovingkindness is good; turn to me according to the multitude of Your tender mercies.

GOD IS GOOD TO THE PURE IN HEART.
Ps 73:1 Truly God is good to Israel, to such as are pure in heart.

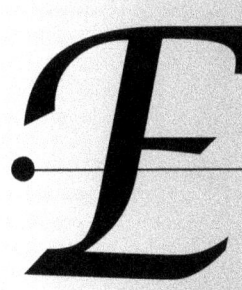# Empowering Nine Proven Giving Keys

GOD WILL NOT WITHHOLD ANY GOOD THING FROM YOU.
Ps 84:11 For the Lord God is a sun and shield; the Lord will give grace and glory; no good thing will He withhold from those who walk uprightly.

GOD WILL GIVE YOU GOOD THINGS AND INCREASE YOUR BUSINESS.
Ps 85:12 Yes, the Lord will give what is good; and our land will yield its increase.

GOD IS ABUNDANT IN MERCY TOWARD YOU.
Ps 86:5 For You, Lord, are good, and ready to forgive, and abundant in mercy to all those who call upon You.

GOD IS GOOD.
Ps 100:5 For the Lord is good; His mercy is everlasting, and His truth endures to all generations.

GOD IS GOOD AND HE DOES GOOD.
Ps 119:68 You are good, and do good; teach me Your statutes.

GOD GIVES GOOD GIFTS TO YOU.
Matt 7:11 If you then, being evil, know how to give good gifts to your children, how much more will your Father who is in heaven give good things to those who ask Him!

A HEART FULL OF GOD'S GOODNESS WILL BE A HEART THAT GIVES.
Matt 12:35 A good man out of the good treasure of his heart brings forth good things, and an evil man out of the evil treasure brings forth evil things.

GOD IS A GRACIOUS AND COMPASSIONATE GOD.
Ex 33:19 Then He said, "I will make all My goodness pass before you, and I will proclaim the name of the Lord before you. I will be gracious to whom I will be gracious, and I will have compassion on whom I will have compassion."
Ex 34:6 And the Lord passed before him and proclaimed, "The Lord, the Lord God, merciful and gracious, longsuffering, and abounding in goodness and truth."

GOD WILL BLESS YOU.
Ps 21:3 For You meet him with the blessings of goodness; You set a crown of pure gold upon his head.

GOD'S GOODNESS WILL ALWAYS BE WITH YOU.
Ps 23:6 Surely goodness and mercy shall follow me all the days of my life; and I will dwell in the house of the Lord forever.

GOD HAS PREPARED GOOD THINGS FOR YOU.
Ps 31:19 Oh, how great is Your goodness, which You have laid up for those who fear You, which You have prepared for those who trust in You in the presence of the sons of men!

GOD GIVES YOU POWER TO GET WEALTH.
Deut 8:18 And you shall remember the Lord your God, for it is He who gives you power to get wealth, that He may establish His covenant which He swore to your fathers, as it is this day.

GOD GIVES STRENGTH AND POWER TO YOU.
Ps 68:35 O God, You are more awesome than Your holy places. The God of Israel is He who gives strength and power to His people. Blessed be God!

GOD GIVES LIFE TO YOU.
John 6:33 For the bread of God is He who comes down from heaven and gives life to the world.

TRUST IN GOD WHO GIVES YOU ALL THINGS TO ENJOY.
1 Tim 6:17 Command those who are rich in this present age not to be haughty, nor to trust in uncertain riches but in the living God, who gives us richly all things to enjoy.

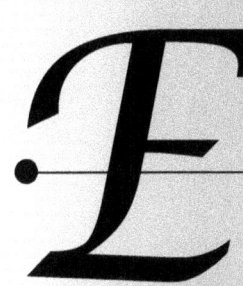

Empowering Nine Proven Giving Keys

GOD HAS THE POWER TO DO ANYTHING.
Isa 40:21-22 Have you not known? Have you not heard? Has it not been told you from the beginning? Have you not understood from the foundations of the earth? It is He who sits above the circle of the earth, and its inhabitants are like grasshoppers, who stretches out the heavens like a curtain, and spreads them out like a tent to dwell in.

GOD HAS THE POWER TO CREATE ANYTHING FROM NOTHING.
Ps 33:6-9 By the word of the Lord the heavens were made, and all the host of them by the breath of His mouth. He gathers the waters of the sea together as a heap; He lays up the deep in storehouses. Let all the earth fear the Lord; let all the inhabitants of the world stand in awe of Him. For He spoke, and it was done; He commanded, and it stood fast.

GOD IS SOVEREIGN AND THERE IS NOTHING TOO HARD FOR HIM.
Jer 32:17-19 Ah, Lord God! Behold, You have made the heavens and the earth by Your great power and outstretched arm. There is nothing too hard for You. You show lovingkindness to thousands, and repay the iniquity of the fathers into the bosom of their children after them—the Great, the Mighty God, whose name is the Lord of hosts. You are great in counsel and mighty in work, for your eyes are open to all the ways of the sons of men, to give everyone according to his ways and according to the fruit of his doings.

Empowering Nine Proven Giving Keys

Scriptural Perspective on Giving

AS YOU GIVE, YOU WILL INCREASE MORE.
Prov 11:24 There is one who scatters, yet increases more; and there is one who withholds more than is right, but it leads to poverty.

AS YOU WATER, YOU WILL BE WATERED MORE.
Prov 11:25 The generous soul will be made rich, and he who waters will also be watered himself.

AS YOU GIVE TO THE POOR, THE LORD PAYS YOU BACK.
Prov 19:17 He who has pity on the poor lends to the Lord, and He will pay back what he has given.

AS YOU ARE FAITHFUL WITH LITTLE, GOD WILL PUT YOU IN CHARGE OF MUCH.
Matt 25:21 His lord said to him, 'Well done, good and faithful servant; you were faithful over a few things, I will make you ruler over many things. Enter into the joy of your lord.'

AS YOU GIVE LIBERALLY, IT WILL BE GIVEN BACK TO YOU RUNNING OVER.
Luke 6:38 Give, and it will be given to you: good measure, pressed down, shaken together, and running over will be put into your bosom. For with the same measure that you use, it will be measured back to you.

THERE WILL BE NO SORROW WITH YOUR WEALTH.
Prov 10:22 The blessing of the Lord makes one rich, and He adds no sorrow with it.

YOUR LIFE WILL BE FILLED WITH PRECIOUS AND PLEASANT RICHES.
Prov 24:3-4 Through wisdom a house is built, and by understanding it is established; by knowledge the rooms are filled with all precious and pleasant riches.

THE LORD WILL ABUNDANTLY BLESS YOUR PROVISIONS.
Ps 132:15 I will abundantly bless her provision; I will satisfy her poor with bread.

YOUR BARNS WILL BE FILLED AND YOUR VATS WILL OVERFLOW.
Prov 3:9-10 Honor the Lord with your possessions, and with the firstfruits of all your increase; so your barns will be filled with plenty, and your vats will overflow with new wine.

AS YOU SOW BOUNTIFULLY, YOU WILL REAP BOUNTIFULLY.
2 Cor 9:6-7 But this I say: He who sows sparingly will also reap sparingly, and he who sows bountifully will also reap bountifully. So let each one give as he purposes in his heart, not grudgingly or of necessity; for God loves a cheerful giver.

AS YOU HAVE GENEROUS EYES, YOU WILL BE BLESSED ABUNDANTLY.
Prov 22:9 He who has a generous eye will be blessed, for he gives of his bread to the poor.

YOU WILL HAVE NO LACK IN YOUR LIFE.
Prov 28:27 He who gives to the poor will not lack, but he who hides his eyes will have many curses.

YOU WILL HAVE HOUSES AND RICHES THAT YOU WILL ENJOY.
Prov 19:14 Houses and riches are an inheritance from fathers, but a prudent wife is from the Lord.

THE WEALTH OF SINNERS IS WAITING FOR YOU.
Prov 13:22 A good man leaves an inheritance to his children's children, but the wealth of the sinner is stored up for the righteous.

Empowering Nine Proven Giving Keys

THE MANY BLESSINGS OF GOD WILL OVERTAKE YOU.
Deut 28:2 And all these blessings shall come upon you and overtake you, because you obey the voice of the Lord your God.

YOU WILL HAVE OPEN WINDOWS OF HEAVEN.
Mal 3:10 "Bring all the tithes into the storehouse, that there may be food in My house, and try Me now in this," says the Lord of hosts, "If I will not open for you the windows of heaven and pour out for you such blessing that there will not be room enough to receive it."

THE LORD WILL GIVE YOU A SURPLUS OF PROSPERITY.
Deut 28:11 And the Lord will grant you plenty of goods, in the fruit of your body, in the increase of your livestock, and in the produce of your ground, in the land of which the Lord swore to your fathers to give you.

GOD WILL MAKE YOUR WAY PROSPEROUS.
Josh 1:8 This book of the law shall not depart from your mouth but you shall meditate in it day and night that you may observe to do according to all that is written in it. For then you will make your way prosperous, and then you will have good success.

YOU WILL SPEND YOUR YEARS IN PROSPERITY AND PLEASURES.
Job 36:11 If they obey and serve Him, they shall spend their days in prosperity, and their years in pleasures.

GOD WILL GIVE YOU THE DREAMS OF YOUR HEART.
Ps 37:4 Delight yourself also in the Lord, and He shall give you the desires of your heart.

WEALTH AND RICHES WILL BE IN YOUR HOUSE.
Ps 112:3 Wealth and riches will be in his house, and his righteousness endures forever.

GOD WILL GIVE YOU TREASURES HIDDEN IN DARKNESS.
Isa 45:3 I will give you the treasures of darkness and hidden riches of secret places, that you may know that I, the Lord, who call you by your name, am the God of Israel.

YOU WILL FIND HIDDEN WEALTH IN SECRET PLACES.
Isa 45:3 I will give you the treasures of darkness and hidden riches of secret places, that you may know that I, the Lord, who call you by your name, am the God of Israel.

YOU WILL ENJOY YOUR SEASONS OF ABUNDANCE.
Phil 4:12 I know how to be abased, and I know how to abound. Everywhere and in all things I have learned both to be full and to be hungry, both to abound and to suffer need.

GOD WILL LIBERALLY SUPPLY ALL YOUR NEEDS.
Phil 4:19 And my God shall supply all your need according to His riches in glory by Christ Jesus.

GOD WILL BLESS YOU EVEN IN A BAD ECONOMY.
Gen 26:3,12 Dwell in this land, and I will be with you and bless you; for to you and your descendants I give all these lands, and I will perform the oath which I swore to Abraham your father... Then Isaac sowed in that land, and reaped in the same year a hundredfold; and the Lord blessed him.

GOD WILL PROVIDE ALL THE SEED YOU NEED TO SOW.
2 Cor 9:10 Now may He who supplies seed to the sower, and bread for food, supply and multiply the seed you have sown and increase the fruits of your righteousness.

YOU WILL NOT LACK ANY GOOD THING.
Ps 34:10 The young lions lack and suffer hunger; but those who seek the Lord shall not lack any good thing.

GOD WILL CROWN YOUR YEAR WITH BOUNTY AND GOODNESS.
Ps 65:11 You crown the year with Your goodness, and Your paths drip with abundance.

Empowering Nine Proven Giving Keys

THE LORD WILL MAKE YOU ABUNDANTLY PROSPEROUS IN YOUR WORK.

Deut 30:9 The Lord your God will make you abound in all the work of your hand, in the fruit of your body, in the increase of your livestock, and in the produce of your land for good. For the Lord will again rejoice over you for good as He rejoiced over your fathers.

THE PROVISIONS OF GOD WILL NEVER RUN OUT.

1 Kings 17:14,16 For thus says the Lord God of Israel: "The bin of flour shall not be used up, nor shall the jar of oil run dry, until the day the Lord sends rain on the earth." … The bin of flour was not used up, nor did the jar of oil run dry, according to the word of the Lord which He spoke by Elijah.

Empowering Nine Proven Giving Keys

#2 The Stewardship Key

Stewardship Definition

The careful and responsible management of something entrusted to one's care. The manager of a hospital or estate; the treasurer of a city. One to whose care or honor one has been entrusted, a curator, a guardian. The word is used to describe the function of delegated responsibility.
(Proverbs 10:4; 13:11; 21:5; Matthew 20:1-16; 25:14-30; Lk 16:1-13; 1 Cor 4:1-2)

Understanding the Biblical Description of a Steward

1. A steward is a manager, administrator, one who governs something properly, rules over something, handles something, takes control of, takes over, takes the helm of, organizes that which is unorganized.

2. Stewards are people who have come to a final conclusion and commitment to God as the owner of all things and accepts the responsibility to manage His resources.

3. Stewards are guardians of the interests of another. A steward owns nothing philosophically, but is careful to guard and protect and increase the property of the one he/she serves.

4. Someone's stewardship of something is the way in which that person controls or organizes it.

5. A steward is one who handles another's property. We are stewards of God's property while we are on earth. He can choose to entrust us with as much or as little as He desires, but in no case will we ever take ownership.

6. A steward is a servant who has been appointed by a ruler to be responsible for the proper direction of the ruler's affairs, for the efficient use of the ruler's resources, and the authority of the ruler's kingdom in the ruler's absence.

> "Choose that employment or calling in which you may be most serviceable to God."
> RICHARD BAXTER

> "Modern church leaders are heirs to greater wealth than the Rockefellers. They are heirs to the kingdom of heaven. Their heavenly Father owns the cattle on a thousands hills and everything in those hills. Those leaders, then, must be aware of their responsibilities to teach the wise use of God's resources. That 'wise use' is called 'stewardship'."
> ELMER TOWNS

Empowering Nine Proven Giving Keys

#3 The Working Key

We were never meant to be idle or inactive. Work was not a result of the fall or the sin of man. We live in a society that is continually bombarding us with the idea of "don't work too hard." As godly men and women, we must ask ourselves if our work habits are an example of the world's attitude of slothfulness or the Bible's admonition of diligence (2 Th 3:10-12).

God Created Man to Work

Man's first commission was to work. God called mankind to cultivate the world He had created and to exercise dominion over it. This was a call to work, to perform both manual labor—pruning trees, tilling the fields—and intellectual labor—naming the animals (Genesis 2:17).

The 21st Century and the Degeneration of Work

When man degenerates, so do his habits of work, his motives for work and his enthusiasm for work. When society degenerates, so do its ideas, vision and basic principles of work. The Bible, however, teaches clear principles and attitudes for the Christian (Col 3:23-24; Eph 6:5-8; 1 Tim 6:1-3; 2 Thess 3:1-10; Eph 4:28-29).

The Biblical Description of a Sluggard from Proverbs

A sluggard is a person who has good intentions but does not give himself to the daily responsibilities that bring prosperity and fruitfulness. This person is the opposite of a diligent person.

1. The sluggard neglects preparation for the future. (Pr 6:6-11).
2. The sluggard lives in poverty (Pr 10:4).
3. The sluggard brings his/her parents to shame (Pr 10:5).
4. The sluggard is a source of irritation to co-workers (Pr 10:26).
5. The sluggard is a slave to others (Pr 12:24).
6. The sluggard desires better things but is too lazy to work to receive them (Pr 13:4; 21:25-26).
7. The sluggard is a big talker but never does anything (Pr 14:23).
8. The sluggard is always having problems (Pr 15:19).
9. The sluggard is destroying his/her own life (Pr 18:9).

Empowering Nine Proven Giving Keys

10. The sluggard's laziness makes him or her ineffective (Pr 19:15).
11. The sluggard starts something but doesn't finish it (Pr 19:24).
12. The sluggard is always asking help of others (Pr 20:4).
13. The sluggard justifies laziness (Pr 22:13; 26:13).
14. The sluggard deceives himself (Pr 26:16).
15. The sluggard follows empty pursuits (Pr 28:19).

The Biblical Description of a Diligent Person from Proverbs

A diligent person is one who applies himself, gives attention to the needs of life, looks to the future and is willing to put forth effort and hard work (Pr 10:4; 12:24).

Empowering Nine Proven Giving Keys

#4 The Giving Key

Giving Definition

To give is to yield control or possession of something, surrendering it. To yield oneself and one's possessions without restraint or control. To bestow, confer, impart, grant, or deliver. To put into the possession of another for his use.

Giving The Tithe

Tithe is the tenth part of anything. It is the first part of our income, the first part of all we earn, and it already belongs to the Lord. This is our first giving responsibility and our minimum financial commitment.

Sir John Templeton, chairman of a $15 billion fund, said, "I have watched over 100,000 families over my years of investment counseling. I always saw greater prosperity and happiness among those families who tithed than those who didn't."

Giving The Offering

An offering is an undesignated, unlimited amount given as a free-will love gift unto the Lord. We are encouraged in Scripture to grow in the grace of giving. Tithe remains always the tithe, 10%, but offerings are unlimited giving. This is where we grow in liberality, generosity, faith and sacrifice (Luke 6:38; 2 Corinthians 9:7).

Rick Warren says that giving benefits. Giving makes me more like God. Giving draws me closer to God. Giving breaks the grip of materialism. Giving strengthens my faith. Giving is an investment for eternity. Giving blesses me in return. Giving makes me happy.

> "The tithe is a wonderful goal, but a terrible place to stop."
> BILL HYBELS

Empowering Nine Proven Giving Keys

#5 The Receiving Key

Receiving Definition

To receive is to obtain something; come into possession of; to take a thing offered; taking; accepting; admitting; embracing.

The principle of receiving is scriptural, as is the principle of reaping. Reaping is receiving, reaping is fulfillment, reaping is finishing the course, reaping is the receiver's reward. All seed will produce more than what is planted, so it is in God's economy. We plant the seed; life and work waters the seed; but God gives the increase.

The Attitude of a Receiver

The attitude of receiving is to take and receive with open hands, by faith making room for and receiving by deliberate and ready reception of all that God is bringing into your hands (Matthew 7:8; John 16:24).

Ways In Which A Believer Receives

Receive from your work or business

Receive from your wise decisions and investments

Receive from surprise blessings and hidden protections

God will withhold no good thing from us (Psalm 84:11)

The Receiver Believes the Promises

The promise is a pledge, a word of honor, a vow, oath, warranty, guarantee, covenant. It is the ground for hope, expectation, assurance of eventual success (Romans 4:20).

The Promiser is God and His Word (Numbers 23:19; Hebrews 6:18).

The Promises Concerning Our Finances (Proverbs 11:24-25; 19:17).

The Receiver's Commitment

A commitment to enlarging my prayers and my asking

A commitment to living by faith and not by sight

A commitment to standing in times of testing

A commitment to rejoicing as I see the provision on its way

Empowering Nine Proven Giving Keys

#6 The Managing Key

God evaluates us as servants using His resources, not as owners using our own money and resources. Since all we do should glorify His name and extend His work on earth, how we go about using His money is crucial. It is the quality of financial management, not the quantity of finances managed. Godly biblical money management is a matter of how and not how much. It's not how much money you make but what you do with the money you have (2 Timothy 1:7; Proverbs 16:32; Joshua 1:8; Psalm 1:1-3; Luke 16:1-13; Matthew 25:14-30).

God Uses Money To Teach Us
- To establish a dependence on the Lord and to trust Him.
- To develop a spirit of gratefulness and contentment.
- To teach us to live within our means.
- To help us enjoy our life, possessions and blessings.
- To give us direction by having or not having sufficient resources.
- To determine who is the Lord of our life.
- To manifest His supernatural power to us.
- To deliver us from wrong motives and attitudes, He will take money from us.

What Is Financial Freedom
Financial freedom is an attitude. Our attitude must be to use our resources to serve God, His church and others, not just to comfort myself. Financial Freedom is a decision and a discipline (Luke 12:17-19).

Scriptural Facts About My Finances
- You cannot take your possessions with you (Luke 12:17-19).
- You can know who you serve by how you use your money (Le 16:13).
- Greed is a life destroyer (Luke 11:39; Proverbs 1:19; 15:27).
- God expects you to handle your money wisely (Mt 25:21,23; Pr 10:5).
- You are responsible for all your decisions (Galatians 6:7-8).
- We should plan with difficulties in mind (Eccl 7:14; Pr 22:3).

Empowering Nine Proven Giving Keys

Managing Begins With Developing New Habits

- Adjust living habits and make new plans for your personal budget (1 Cor 9:27).
- Make small priority shifts in your life beginning now (Job 8:7).
- Get rid of unnecessary, expensive toys
- Reexamine your life insurance
- Either control or destroy your credit cards

Empowering Nine Proven Giving Keys

#7 The Releasing Key

The local church and the overseeing leadership must cultivate a biblical vision for those who are called to the marketplace. The businessperson is a vital key to spreading the gospel in the secular setting and to being a blessing to the local church. Business people usually have the gifts of faith, giving and leadership. These people need to be encouraged, challenged, accepted, respected, released and pastored.

The Christian Businessperson

The Christian businessperson is a sign of the kingdom of God in this present world, called to cultivate a distinctiveness that points to the world's future and to live and work in the world's presence, called to be light, showing the life of the kingdom to the world, as salt permeating the world, a reflection of godly eternal values in the world and to the world (1 Chronicles 4:10).

True Success Is

True success is fulfilling the purposes for which God has created you. It is accomplishing the dreams God has had for you from before the foundations of the world. True success is a journey, a gradual process, avoiding extremes that damage biblical values and balanced living (Isaiah 55:8-11).

The Business Person and a Biblical Philosophy of Success

- ♦ We are to extend the kingdom of God. We are to live with a goal toward excellence and an attitude of achievement toward biblical success, biblical values and biblical priorities (Proverbs 3:6).

- ♦ We are to adopt the early Protestant or Puritan work ethic. This is a simple view in which the average person believes his or her work not only matters but contributes to a sense of community and integrity in all of life (2 Thess 3:6-10).

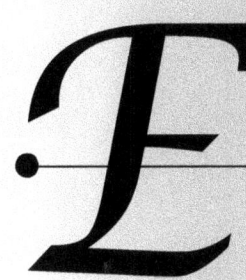

Empowering Nine Proven Giving Keys

- We must adopt the view that it is our Christian duty to transcend mediocrity in our daily routines and to link our work in the world with our service to an all-knowing God of excellence who desires believers to work with excellence and achieve success in our area of responsibility. This is our divine calling (Eph 6:5-8; 2 Timothy 1:9).

- We must adopt the biblical view that God has a destiny for me which He has known in advance and is wisely directing my life toward. This destiny involves my calling to be a success in my work. My everyday ordinary life has within it seeds of greatness (Eph 4:1; Rom 8:28-30).

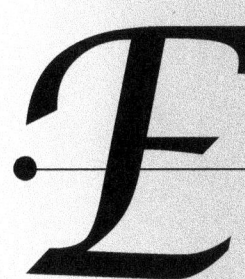

Empowering Nine Proven Giving Keys

#8 The Prospering Key

Definition of Prosperity

To succeed, to be profitable; to have a vision, to see clearly; to accomplish successfully, to reach the intended goal, to finish well.
(Genesis 24:40,42; Genesis 26:13; 39:3,23; Deuteronomy 30:5)

Biblical View of Success

- True success is a journey, a gradual process, avoiding extremes that damage biblical values: home, health, friendship and a godly character. True success abides in a realm in which balanced living is achieved.
(Proverbs 18:11; Ecclesiastes 5:10)

- True success is the progressive realization of predetermined, worthwhile godly goals which have been stabilized with balance and purified belief.
(Matthew 6:26)

- True success is accomplished when a person continually applies the basic principles of godly living to his life.
(3 John 2; Romans 12:1-2)

The Posture Toward Godly Success
(Psalm 1:3; Proverbs 28:13; Isaiah 54:17)

- Pursing Godly Success Through Specific Praying

- Positioning for Godly Success Through Common Sense Disciplines and Habits

- Positioning for Godly Success by Honoring the Basics

Empowering Nine Proven Giving Keys

Insights of Successful People
(1 Chronicles 22:11; 2 Chronicles 20:20; 26:5)

Joseph: Allowing God to turn misfortunes into benefits by holding on to your dreams, your integrity, your attitude, and your course.
(Genesis 39:2-23)

Joshua: Following the directions, principles and patterns found in the word of God through meditation, observation and detailed obedience at all times.
(Joshua 1:8-9)

Uzziah: Gaining godly insights through diligent fasting and prayer, thus resisting the pull to lesser priorities.
(2 Chronicles 26:5; 31:21)

Paul: Handling successfully the many storms, setbacks and vicious trials that seek to blow us off our course to true success.
(Romans 1:10; Acts 27-28)

Nehemiah: Willing to give up the security and comfort of a great job to go and do something significant for someone else.
(Nehemiah 1:11; 2:20)

Empowering Nine Proven Giving Keys

#9 The Bequeathing Key

Inheritance Definition

The act of inheriting, something inherited or to be inherited, something regarded as a heritage. Heritage is property that is or can be inherited, something that is passed down from preceding generations, a tradition.

Bequeathing is something passed from one generation to another. It could be called a heritage, legacy, tradition, birthright, family possession, estate, bequest, money or goods left to one's heirs.

Eight Ways to Create a Legacy

- Specific bequest: transfer a specific piece of property.

- General bequest: transfer a stated sum of money.

- Contingent bequest: require a certain event to occur before the bequest is given.

- Residuary bequest: transfers whatever is left of your estate after other matters have been taken care of.

- Unrestricted bequest: allows the beneficiaries to use the funds as they desire.

- Restricted bequest: allows you to specify how the funds will be used.

- Endowed bequest: allows only the interest income from your gift to be used; the principal must remain untouched.

- Memorial bequest: given in the memory of a person.

Empowering the Giving of Tithes and Offerings

SESSION #3

> The tithes and offerings are the foundational giving stones in every local church. The leader is to pastor and to preach these two giving stones in a powerful and practical manner. The preaching of the word is the primary means by which truth is established. The pastoring of a truth is equally important and must be done with wisdom, patience and faith. The tithe is a God-idea and a good idea. It is a foundational doctrine that can release a church into a steady flow of released resources for the fulfillment of vision and mission. Offerings are God-ordained to allow the Holy Spirit to direct people into the many "giving doors" the leadership has established.

Empowering the Giving of Tithes and Offerings

I. Cultivating The Heart of a Giving Church
(2 Timothy 4:2)

   A. The Work of Plowing with Preaching the Word
       (Psalm 119:130; Acts 17:11; 2 Corinthians 9:10)

   B. The Wisdom of Sowing with Preaching the Word
       (Jeremiah 3:15; Colossians 3:16; 1 Thessalonians 2:13; Isaiah 55:10-11)

   C. The Patience of Reaping with Preaching the Word
       (Psalm 126:6; 1 Corinthians 3:6; 2 Timothy 2:24-25)

II. The Preacher and The Word

   A. Preaching is the Leader's Responsibility

       1. 1 Timothy 2:7 "For which I was appointed a preacher and an apostle—I am speaking the truth in Christ and not lying—a teacher of the Gentiles in faith and truth."

       2. 2 Timothy 2:15 "Be diligent to present yourself approved to God, a worker who does not need to be ashamed, rightly dividing the word of truth."

       3. 2 Timothy 4:2 "Preach the word! Be ready in season and out of season. Convince, rebuke, exhort, with all longsuffering and teaching."

       4. Colossians 1:28 "Him we preach, warning every man and teaching every man in all wisdom, that we may present every man perfect in Christ Jesus."

       5. Acts 6:4 "But we will give ourselves continually to prayer and to the ministry of the word."

> "The Bible is alive - it speaks to me. It has feet - it runs after me. It has hands - it lays hold of me."
> MARTIN LUTHER

> "Preaching is to exhort in a tedious and tiresome manner, to preach the Bible, not just about the Bible, but preaching the word."

Empowering the Giving of Tithes and Offerings

  6. 2 Timothy 3:16 "All Scripture is given by inspiration of God, and is profitable for doctrine, for reproof, for correction, for instruction in righteousness."

  7. Isaiah 2:3 "Many people shall come and say, 'Come, and let us go up to the mountain of the Lord, to the house of the God of Jacob; He will teach us His ways, and we shall walk in His paths.' For out of Zion shall go forth the law, and the word of the Lord from Jerusalem."

 B. The Early Church Preached the Word

  1. Acts 5:42 "And daily in the temple, and in every house, they did not cease teaching and preaching Jesus as the Christ."

  2. Acts 6:7 "Then the word of God spread, and the number of the disciples multiplied greatly in Jerusalem, and a great many of the priests were obedient to the faith."

  3. Acts 11:26 "And when he had found him, he brought him to Antioch. So it was that for a whole year they assembled with the church and taught a great many people. And the disciples were first called Christians in Antioch."

  4. Acts 15:35 "Paul and Barnabas also remained in Antioch, teaching and preaching the word of the Lord, with many others also."

  5. Acts 20:20 "How I kept back nothing that was helpful, but proclaimed it to you, and taught you publicly and from house to house."

  6. Acts 28:31 "...Preaching the kingdom of God and teaching the things which concern the Lord Jesus Christ with all confidence, no one forbidding him."

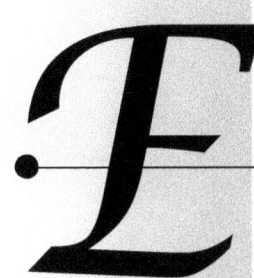

Empowering the Giving of Tithes and Offerings

    7.   Acts 13:1 "Now in the church that was at Antioch there were certain prophets and teachers: Barnabas, Simeon who was called Niger, Lucius of Cyrene, Manaen who had been brought up with Herod the tetrarch, and Saul."

    8.   1 Corinthians 12:28 "And God has appointed these in the church: first apostles, second prophets, third teachers, after that miracles, then gifts of healings, helps, administrations, varieties of tongues."

III. The Word of God

    A.   Hebrews 4:12

New King James: "For the word of God is living and powerful, and sharper than any two-edged sword, piercing even to the division of soul and spirit, and of joints and marrow, and is a discerner of the thoughts and intents of the heart."

Amplified Bible: "For the Word that God speaks is alive and full of power [making it active, operative, energizing, and effective]; it is sharper than any two-edged sword, penetrating to the dividing line of the breath of life (soul) and [the immortal] spirit, and of joints and marrow [of the deepest parts of our nature], exposing and sifting and analyzing and judging the very thoughts and purposes of the heart."

The Message: "His powerful word is sharp as a surgeon's scalpel, cutting through everything, whether doubt or defense, laying us open to listen and obey. Nothing and no one is impervious to God's word. We can't get away from it—no matter what."

    1.   The written word of God cannot be taken lightly. If the listeners do not obey the word, they come face to face with God himself.
(Jn 10:35; Luke 16:17; 2 Timothy 3:16; Romans 3:2; Acts 7:38)

    2.   The written word of God reflects the true character of God Himself, the source of all life. The word of God is living, full of life, full of energy to achieve the declared end. A revelation that is living has a constant application to the minds of the recipients.
(John 6:66; 1 Peter 1:23; Acts 7:38)

3. The written word preached becomes a sharp knife that cuts deeply like a skillful surgeon, cutting away the diseases of the flesh.
(Ephesians 6:17; Revelation 1:16; Isaiah 49:2)

B. Ten Descriptions of the Word of God from Psalm 119

1. The law: to direct, guide, teach, make straight, point forward.

2. Statutes: to mark, trace out, describe and ordain.

3. Precepts: to take notice or care of a thing, attend, have respect to, appoint, visit.

4. Commandments: to command, ordain, order.

5. Testimonies: beyond, further, bear witness.

6. Judgements: to judge, determine, regulate, order and discern.

7. Truth: to make steady, constant, settle, trust, believe.

8. Word: to speak intelligently, utter one's sentiments, any prophecy or immediate communication from heaven, the word of Yahweh.

9. Ways: to proceed, go on, walk, treat.

10. Righteousness: to do justice, to give full weight; that which teaches a man to give to all their due (God, man, himself), for every man has duties to God, his neighbor and himself to perform.

C. The leader must have confidence in the word of God on all subjects, especially finances. The preacher must believe the word will bless and add to, not take away from, the people.
(Psalm 119:1-2,12; 1:1; 32:1-2; 34:8; 65:4; 89:4-5; 94:12)

Empowering the Giving of Tithes and Offerings

Psalm 119:1-8 (The Message Bible)
"You're blessed when you stay on course, walking steadily on the road revealed by God. You're blessed when you follow his directions, doing your best to find him. That's right—you don't go off on your own; you walk straight along the road he set. You, God, prescribed the right way to live; now you expect us to live it. Oh, that my steps might be steady, keeping to the course you set; then I'd never have any regrets in comparing my life with your counsel. I thank you for speaking straight from your heart; I learn the pattern of your righteous ways. I'm going to do what you tell me to do; don't ever walk off and leave me."

IV. Preach Tithing With Conviction, Confidence and Clarity

A. Preaching to Enlighten the Giver <u>About the Conflict Within Them</u>
(Galatians 2:20; Romans 6:6; 7:14-25; Galatians 4:7)

Our old man is the sum total of everything we inherit from Adam and reflects everything in our life which is outside the new. The old nature is stubborn, delights in sin and condones sin.

1. The Old Man is Selfish and Self-Serving

   a. I am carnal, unspiritual, and made of flesh that is frail.
      (Romans 7:14)
      - It is I who am sensual (Norlie)
      - But I am unspiritual (JB, Weymouth)
      - But I am earthly (TCNT)
      - I am made of flesh that is frail (Williams)
      - And I am fleshly (Young)
      - Bought and sold under the dominion of sin (Montgomery)

   b. I don't understand my own actions.
      (Romans 7:15)
      - For what I work I know not (Panin)
      - What I perform (Alford)
      - What I accomplish (Worrell)
      - I do not understand my own actions (RSV)
      - I do not practice what I would (Wesley)
      - What I work out, I do not approve (Wilson)
      - I don't always do what I really want to do (SEB)

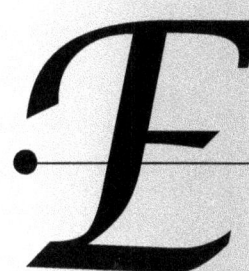

Empowering the Giving of Tithes and Offerings

    c. What I want to do, I don't practice.
       (Romans 7:15)
- What I want to do, I don't practice, but instead what I hate is exactly what I do (Adams)
- I do not act according to my will (HistNT)
- I do what I detest (Moffatt)
- Doing what I actually hate (SEB)
- But what I am averse to is what I do (Weymouth)
- That I habitually do (Montgomery)

    d. What I hate is exactly what I do.
       (Romans 7:15)
- I desire (Alford)
- I intend to do (Montgomery)
- I fail to do (NEB)

    e. It is not all me. There is something else living in me that drives me.
       (Romans 7:18)
- It is no longer I who perform the action (NEB)
- Sin which has its home within me (Weymouth)
- That lodges in me (NEB)

    f. I can will what is right but the power to carry it out is weak.
       (Romans 7:18)
- I can will what is right, but I cannot do it (RSV)
- For though the will to do good is there, the deed is not (NEB)
- To will I find is attainable (HistNT)
- But I am not producing fine things (Adams)
- But not the power of doing what is right (Moffatt)
- The power to carry it out is not (Weymouth)
- But I find no means to perform that (Tyndale)

    g. I don't have the strength to accomplish what is right.
       (Romans 7:18)
- But I do not find the strength to accomplish what is good (Confraternity)
- But to accomplish that which is good (Rheims)
- To avail myself of its benefit? (Fenton)
- But to do it, I find difficult (Campbell)
- But to work the good (Panin)
- The power to do it I do not possess (Barclay)

Empowering the Giving of Tithes and Offerings

      h. I see a pattern. Every time I begin to desire the right things, I am ambushed by an evil attacker. (Romans 7:19)
- When I intend to (Montgomery)
- When I have a will (Douay)
- That every single time I want to (JB)
- When I desire to do that which is good (Alford)
- It is easier for me to do wrong!(TCNT)
- But wrong is all I can manage (Moffatt)
- Is lying in ambush for me (Weymouth)
- Is always in my way (Williams)
- Evil is controlling me (SEB)
- Close at hand (PNT)

      i. I am weary of fighting this inward battle with the law of sin warring against my soul and my body, bringing me into captivity as a prisoner of sin. (Romans 7:23)
- Battling against the principles which my reason dictates (Berkeley)
- Rebelling against (Geneva)
- Fighting against (Douay)
- Operated by (Williams)
- And holding me captive (Adams)
- It is making me a prisoner to the sinful law (SEB)
- Making me a prisoner of war (Wuest)
- And captivating me (Scarlett, Wesley)

    2. The New Nature is Giving and God-Serving
(Rom 1:16-17; 2 Corinthians 4:16; 5:17; Colossians 3:10)

Our new man embraces everything which flows newly from the Lord at our regeneration.

      a. Our new man loves to pray and worship.
      b. Our new man loves righteousness and purity.
      c. Our new man loves the word of God.
      d. Our new man loves to serve and help.
      e. Our new man loves to give and give liberally.

B. Preaching to Enlighten the Giver <u>About the Truth of Tithing</u>

    1. Tithe is the <u>first</u> of our wages and the <u>first</u> of our increase.
(Deuteronomy 26:10; Proverbs 3:9-10)

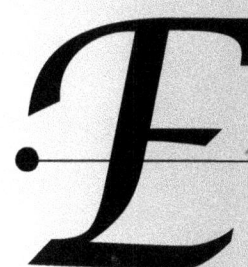mpowering the Giving of Tithes and Offerings

2. Tithe is the <u>acknowledgement</u> that all we have belongs to the Lord.
   (Deuteronomy 26:10; Genesis 28:22; Deuteronomy 8:11-20)

3. Tithe is to be given with an <u>attitude</u> of <u>worship</u> as a rejoicing offering.
   (Deuteronomy 26:10; 2 Cor 9:7; John 12:3-5; Lev 22:17-22,29)

4. Tithe is to be given from our <u>increase</u> also.
   (Deuteronomy 26:12)

5. Tithe is the <u>sacred portion</u> that we set aside as the Lord's. It is holy.
   (Deuteronomy 26:13; Leviticus 27:26-33)

6. Tithe is not to be used for <u>personal needs</u>.
   (Deuteronomy 26:14; Leviticus 27:30)

7. Tithe is to be given as an act of <u>spiritual obedience</u>.
   (Deuteronomy 26:14)

8. Tithe is one aspect that <u>has promised blessings</u> that can affect our lives.
   (Deuteronomy 26:15; 26:19; Malachi 3:8-11; Luke 6:38)

9. Tithe is the <u>provision</u> for the <u>releasing</u> of ministry in the house of the Lord.
   (Nehemiah 13:10-12; 1 Corinthians 9:9; Acts 28:10)

10. Tithing is not just <u>Old Testament teaching</u>; both Jesus and the Apostles confirmed tithing and offerings.
    (Matthew 23:23; 6:1; 1 Corinthians 16:1-2)

11. Tithing is a <u>biblical minimum</u> and will not limit our giving but open the door to a genuine stewardship.

Empowering the Giving of Tithes and Offerings

12. Tithing is the <u>acknowledgement</u> of <u>ownership</u> that God is owner of all and I am only a steward or trustee over my human estate.

13. Tithing is a <u>token of consecration</u> that one has surrendered all and made Him Lord.

C. Preaching to Enlighten the Giver <u>on How to do Prayer-Warfare for their Tithe</u>
(Malachi 3:8-9)

1. Repent of withholding and removing the blessing blockage.
(Malachi 3:8-9)

   a. Robbery means taking either by fraud or violent that which belongs to another and appropriating it to your own use. It is not only taking what is not yours, but keeping back for yourself what belongs to someone else.
      1) One-tenth belongs to God. Failure to pay that debt is robbery.
      2) Robbing God is permitting something to have stronger power over us than His will.

   b. Men who retain God's money in their treasuries will find it a losing proposition.

2. Bring the tithe into the storehouse.
(Genesis 41:56; Deuteronomy 28:8)

   a. Storehouse: The Old Testament storehouse was the place God designated to keep abundance and to distribute it to the people. It was also His tabernacle where His name was established. Today a storehouse is your local church, the place where you receive your spiritual food, nurturing, and fellowship, the place you call home.

   b. God issues an invitation to prove the Lord's promises, to test God. He virtually offers a guaranteed direct and abundant return on your investment.

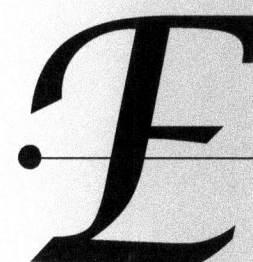

Empowering the Giving of Tithes and Offerings

    3.   Stand with the promises of God for the tithe.
(Proverbs 10:6; 28:20; Malachi 3:10; Genesis 12:2)

        a.   Blessings multiply.

        b.   Open the shut windows of heaven.

        c.   Pour out a personalized, custom-made blessing.

        d.   Enlarge your blessing beyond your capacity to receive.
(Psalm 132:15; Proverbs 10:22)

        e.   Blessings upon your work.
(Deuteronomy 15:10; Ecclesiastes 2:9-11)

        f.   The Lord will rebuke the devourer.
(Malachi 3:11; 13:4)

        g.   Stand with the authority of God for continued blessings.

V. Preaching To Encourage the Giving of Freewill Offerings

    A.   The Freewill Offering – The giving of our offering is an undesignated, unlimited amount given as a free-will love gift to the Lord.

        A faith harvest offering is given by the believer with the knowledge that this seed is sowed in faith, believing God to water it and enable it to become the full harvest of what God desires to bring into my life. This is a faith offering, a specific giving with liberality and sacrifice. *(At City Bible Church we have a faith harvest offering annually.)*

        1.   A faith harvest offering is given out of a willing heart.
(Ezra 1:4; Ezra 7:16; Ps 96:8; Exodus 25:2; 35:5)

        2.   A faith harvest offering is given out of a stirring of the Holy Spirit.
(Exodus 35:21)

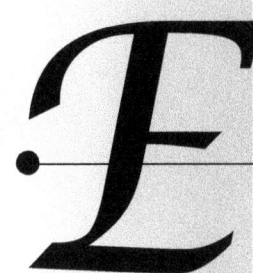# Empowering the Giving of Tithes and Offerings

       3.   A faith harvest offering is given out of my own special treasure.
(1 Chronicles 29:3)

       4.   A faith harvest offering is a sacrificial offering.
(2 Samuel 24:24; Mark 12:41-44; 2 Corinthians 8:3)

       5.   A faith harvest offering is motivated by grace not guilt, competition or pressure.
(2 Corinthians 8:1; 9:7-8)

       6.   A faith harvest offering is a seed-faith offering.
(II Corinthians 9:6; Genesis 8:22; Psalm 126:6; Galatians 6:9; Hebrews 11:6; Matthew 17:20)

  B.   The leader should open the multiple "doors" for giving offerings.
(Deuteronomy 16:7; 2 Corinthians 9:7)

       1.   When we choose not to use a door of ministry, we lose the opportunity. You don't know who has money in their pockets until you ask for it. Once a pocket is opened, it is easier to open it again. If you don't provide the cause, someone else will get into their pocket. God gives us people according to our vision and commitment.

       2.   God calls everyone to begin with the tithe and offerings. The tithe is not deregulated giving, but offerings can be. The more diverse a church is in its overall ministry, the more people will tithe, thus supporting these ministries and giving special offering toward specific ministries. There are dollars in people's pockets that will never be given if they do not have the opportunity to go through the door for which they have a specific burden.

       3.   The giving doors philosophy should not negate a foundational philosophy of "first the tithe" for the overall established vision of the church. The vision for the house must not be belittled and special ministries exalted above where they should be.

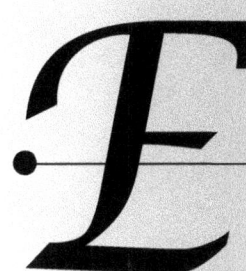

Empowering the Giving of Tithes and Offerings

C. The Giving Doors Possibilities

The giving doors should be defined and communicated.

1. The door of giving to the poor

2. The door of giving to children's needs

3. The door of giving to debt retirement

4. The door of giving to world missions

5. The door of giving to church planting

6. The door of giving to strategic, creative evangelism

7. The door of giving to new building construction

8. The door of giving to education (Christian schools and colleges)

9. The door of giving to purchase new equipment

10. The door of giving to capital improvements

11. The door of giving to inheritance and wills

12. The door of giving to the community needs (pregnancy centers, counseling, child abuse)

Empowering the Giving of Tithes and Offerings

VII. Scriptures and Prayers When Receiving Tithes and Offerings

1. As I give in today's offering, I stand on God's promises that the Lord will cause His blessings to come upon me as the windows of heaven are opened.

   MALACHI 3:10 "Bring all the tithes into the storehouse, that there may be food in My house, and try Me now in this," says the Lord of hosts, "If I will not open for you the windows of heaven and pour out for you such blessing that there will not be room enough to receive it."

2. As I give in today's offering, I believe that the Lord will cause the enemies who rise up against me to be defeated as He rebukes the devourer on my behalf.

   MALACHI 3:11 "And I will rebuke the devourer for your sakes, so that he will not destroy the fruit of your ground, nor shall the vine fail to bear fruit for you in the field," says the Lord of hosts.

3. As I give in today's offering, I stand on the word of God and believe the promise that as I sow my seed, God will water my seed and multiply my seed according to His greatness and goodness.

   2 CORINTHIANS 9:6 "But this I say: He who sows sparingly will also reap sparingly, and he who sows bountifully will also reap bountifully."

   2 CORINTHIANS 9:10 "Now may He who supplies seed to the sower… supply and multiply the seed you have."

4. As I give in today's offering, I rejoice as I bring to the Lord the firstfruits of my income and my increase, I worship the Lord with a grateful heart, for He has provided faithfully for me and my house. I give willingly and cheerfully.

   DEUTERONOMY 26:10 "And now, I have brought the firstfruits of the land which you, O Lord, have given me." Then you shall set it before the Lord your God, and worship before the Lord your God.

5. As I give in today's offering, I pray that God will guard my path and help me to walk in His ways and obey His principles all the days of my life, let my life be fruitful and impacting.

   PSALMS 1:1-3 "Blessed is the man who walks not in the counsel of the ungodly, nor stands in the path of sinners, nor sits in the seat of the scornful; but his delight is in the law of the Lord, and in His law he meditates day and night. He shall be like a tree planted by the rivers of water, that brings forth its fruit in its season, whose leaf also shall not wither; and whatever he does shall prosper."

Empowering the Giving of Tithes and Offerings

6. | As I give in today's offering, I believe that you, O Lord, are a loving, kind, gentle, giving, generous, and liberal God, you will not hold back any good thing for my life, you are my provider. | PSALMS 34:8-10 "Oh, taste and see that the Lord is good; blessed is the man who trusts in Him! … Those who seek the Lord shall not lack any good thing"

7. | As I give in today's offering, I affirm that all the tithe belongs to the Lord and is holy. I have willingly set aside this sacred part of my income according to His word and by faith and obedience I now bring my tithe into the storehouse, my local church. | LEVITICUS 27:30 "And all the tithe of the land … is the Lord's. It is holy to the Lord."

MALACHI 3:10 "Bring all the tithes into the storehouse, that there may be food in My house, and try Me now in this," says the Lord of hosts, "If I will not open for you the windows of heaven and pour out for you such blessing that there will not be room enough to receive it."

8. | As I give in today's offering, I acknowledge that God has supreme dominion and universal authority, and I am dependent on the grace and power of almighty God.

I am a visitor, a sojourner on this planet, a steward of what God allows me to manage. God is rightful owner of all things. | 1 CHRONICLES 29:11-15 "Yours, O Lord, is the greatness, the power and the glory, the victory and the majesty; for all that is in heaven and in earth is Yours; Yours is the kingdom, O Lord, and You are exalted as head over all. Both riches and honor come from You, and You reign over all. In Your hand is power and might; in Your hand it is to make great and to give strength to all. Now therefore, our God, we thank You and praise Your glorious name. But who am I, and who are my people, that we should be able to offer so willingly as this? For all things come from You, and of Your own we have given You. For we are aliens and pilgrims before You, as were all our fathers; our days on earth are as a shadow, and without hope."

9. | As I give in today's offering, I stand on the reliability of God's word. God's word is perfect, trustworthy and supernatural. It is God's voice into my life. I believe God's promises in the scriptures are for me, and by faith I claim them. | NUMBERS 23:19 "God is not a man, that He should lie, nor a son of man, that He should repent. Has He said, and will He not do? Or has He spoken, and will He not make it good?"

Empowering the Giving of Tithes and Offerings

10. | As I give in today's offering, I rejoice in all the numerous and miraculous blessings God has given to me—more blessings than I could have ever dreamed of, more blessings than I deserve, more blessings than I can count, blessings over every area of my life. I rejoice! | PSALM 103:1-5 "Bless the Lord, O my soul; and all that is within me, bless His holy name! Bless the Lord, O my soul, and forget not all His benefits: Who forgives all your iniquities, Who heals all your diseases, Who redeems your life from destruction, Who crowns you with lovingkindness and tender mercies, Who satisfies your mouth with good things, so that your youth is renewed like the eagle's."

11. | As I give in today's offering, I believe that God desires to give me seed to sow and multiply my harvest. I believe that in God all things are possible at any time in any environment. By faith I receive today all that God desires to release in and through my hands to extend His Kingdom. | LUKE 6:38 "Give, and it will be given to you: good measure, pressed down, shaken together, and running over will be put into your bosom. For with the same measure that you use, it will be measured back to you."

12. | As I give in today's offering, I acknowledge that my life consists of more than the things I have or the things I desire. My life finds meaning in Christ and in His eternal kingdom. My life is to be lived as a person who knows where to put my treasures. My giving of my money is an investment into ministry that touches people for eternal destinies. | MATTHEW 6:19-21 "Do not lay up for yourselves treasures on earth, where moth and rust destroy and where thieves break in and steal; but lay up for yourselves treasures in heaven, where neither moth nor rust destroys and where thieves do not break in and steal. For where your treasure is, there your heart will be also."

13. | As I give in today's offering, I have vision to see beyond my present circumstances, beyond my present problems or crises, beyond my needs and my desires. By faith, I see my God working on my behalf to open doors that have been shut, to open up my mind to new ideas and my heart to new passions. I give today with great expectation for my God to do the impossible. | 2 CORINTHIANS 5:7 "For we walk by faith, not by sight."

1 CORINTHIANS 16:13 "Watch, stand fast in the faith, be brave, be strong."

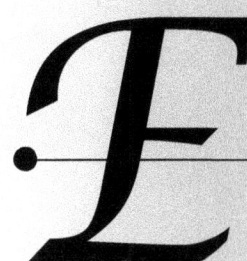

Empowering the Giving of Tithes and Offerings

14. As I give in today's offering, I stand in unity with God, His word and the Holy Spirit. I stand together in prayer and agreement with those in my house, believing God will do exceedingly, abundantly above all that I could ask or imagine. I stand with my shield and my sword to war against doubt and unbelief. I stand against all the powers of the enemy. I stand in my place and will not be moved. I will not give up!

    EPHESIANS 6:11, 13 "Put on the whole armor of God, that you may be able to stand against the wiles of the devil… Therefore take up the whole armor of God, that you may be able to withstand in the evil day and having done all to stand."

    2 CHRONICLES 20:17 "You will not need to fight in this battle. Position yourselves, stand still and see the salvation of the Lord, who is with you, O Judah and Jerusalem! Do not fear or be dismayed; tomorrow go out against them, for the Lord is with you."

15. As I give in today's offering, I have faith in the God who created the heavens and the earth, the God who has given us His infallible word, the God who promises and never breaks His word. I have faith in my God who shall supply all that is needed, when it is needed. He is never late and never early, but always on time every time. I choose to put my trust in the Lord again today, right now.

    ROMANS 12:3 "For I say, through the grace given to me, to everyone who is among you, not to think of himself more highly than he ought to think, but to think soberly, as God has dealt to each one a measure of faith."

    HEBREWS 11:6 "Without faith it is impossible to please Him, for he who comes to God must believe that He is, and that He is a rewarder of those who diligently seek Him."

16. As I give in today's offering, I commit myself to the written word of God. I seek to obey His word and to put it into practice, not excusing myself by my own reasoning. I choose to honor His word above my thoughts, desires or arguments. God deserves my respect and obedience. I give today with an obedient spirit and attitude.

    ISAIAH 1:19 "If you are willing and obedient, you shall eat the good of the land."

    PHILIPPIANS 2:8 "And being found in appearance as a man, He humbled Himself and became obedient to the point of death, even the death of the cross."

17. As I give in today's offering, I give thanks to the God of my salvation, to the God who has shown me unmerited mercy and gives me a new heart, a new life and a new destiny. Thank You, Lord, for all Your gracious provisions. I am amazed at how You are watching over every area of my life. I bring my offering this day with a thankful heart.

    PSALM 79:13 "So we, Your people and sheep of Your pasture, will give You thanks forever; we will show forth Your praise to all generations."

    PSALM 106:1 "Praise the Lord! Oh, give thanks to the Lord, for He is good! For His mercy endures forever."

Empowering the Giving of Tithes and Offerings

18. | As I give in today's offering, I willingly give to the Lord, not out of guilt or compulsion, but with a willing heart. I give with a heart that is sincerely excited about the opportunity to give freely and abundantly of all I have, a heart that is soft and easily moved toward the work of God. I love You, Lord. I love Your people, and I love the church where you have placed me. | EXODUS 25:2 "Speak to the children of Israel, that they bring Me an offering. From everyone who gives it willingly with his heart you shall take My offering."

    EXODUS 35:21 "Then everyone came whose heart was stirred, and everyone whose spirit was willing, and they brought the Lord's offering for the work of the tabernacle of meeting, for all its service, and for the holy garments."

    EXODUS 35:5 "Take from among you an offering to the Lord. Whoever is of a willing heart, let him bring it as an offering to the Lord."

19. | As I give in today's offering, I commit myself to walk in the fear of the Lord with humility and sincerity; to respect, honor and obey the Lord God Almighty. I repent of any independent attitude or pride and ask for God to keep me and bless me in every way. I give today with total confidence in my God. | PSALM 19:9 "The fear of the Lord is clean, enduring forever; the judgments of the Lord are true and righteous altogether."

    PSALM 33:8 "Let all the earth fear the Lord; let all the inhabitants of the world stand in awe of Him."

    PSALM 115:11 "You who fear the Lord, trust in the Lord; He is their help and their shield."

    PSALM 115:13 "He will bless those who fear the Lord, both small and great."

20. | As I give in today's offering, I choose to give with a liberal spirit, a liberal heart and an open hand. I will not shrink back because of fear or greed. I will open my hand and give back to the Lord abundantly and generously. I will now allow a stingy spirit to overtake my heart. | ROMANS 12:8 "He who exhorts, in exhortation; he who gives, with liberality; he who leads, with diligence; he who shows mercy, with cheerfulness."

    2 CORINTHIANS 8:2 "…That in a great trial of affliction the abundance of their joy and their deep poverty abounded in the riches of their liberality."

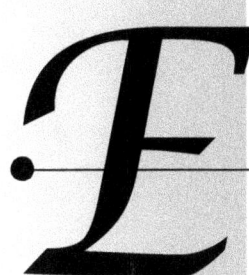

Empowering the Giving of Tithes and Offerings

21. As I give in today's offering, I choose to give with a liberal spirit, a liberal heart, and an open hand. I will not shrink back because or fear or greed. I will open my hand and give back to the Lord abundantly, generously, I will not allow a stingy spirit to overtake my heart.

    ROMANS 12:8 "He who exhorts, in exhortation; he who gives, with liberality; he who leads, with diligence; he who shows mercy, with cheerfulness."

    2 CORINTHIANS 8:2 "That in a great trial of affliction the abundance of their joy and their deep poverty abounded in the riches of their liberality."

22. As I give in today's offering, I resist all thoughts and feelings of anxiety, worry or fear. I confess that I am a child of God. God knows me and loves me. God knows my smallest needs and my largest needs. God is faithful to watch over me like He watches over the birds of the air and the lilies of the field. I joyfully give today with faith and not with fear.

    MATTHEW 6:25-30 "Therefore I say to you, do not worry about your life, what you will eat or what you will drink; nor about your body, what you will put on. Is not life more than food and the body more than clothing? Look at the birds of the air, for they neither sow nor reap nor gather into barns; yet your heavenly Father feeds them. Are you not of more value than they? Which of you by worrying can add one cubit to his stature? So why do you worry about clothing? Consider the lilies of the field, how they grow: they neither toil nor spin; and yet I say to you that even Solomon in all his glory was not arrayed like one of these. Now if God so clothes the grass of the field, which today is, and tomorrow is thrown into the oven, will He not much more clothe you, O you of little faith?"

Empowering the Giving of Tithes and Offerings

EMPOWERING AND RELEASING THE BUSINESS PERSON

SESSION #4

> Business people should be inspired and empowered to fulfill their personal ministry in and through their local church and in the marketplace. It is the responsibility of the church pastoral leadership to enable and equip them. Equipping business people is not just another program; it is a God-right mindset and it is a biblical principle. The releasing of the businessperson into fruitful ministry will enlarge the businessperson and bless the local church. Business people may be a ready vessel for giving liberally to the vision and releasing faith and liberality in others to do the same. This is an important group with every local church that God desires to release into greater ministry.

Empowering and Releasing the Business Person

> "Great minds have purposes; others have wishes."
> WASHINGTON IRVING

I. The Pastor and the Business Person

A. The pastor must have a clear vision for business people.

1. A biblical vision

2. An unselfish vision

3. A spiritual vision

B. The pastor must have a right relationship with the businessperson.

1. A pastoral relationship

2. A transparent relationship

3. A two-way relationship

C. The pastor must have a strategy for the business person.

1. A written-out strategy

2. A progressive, ministry-releasing strategy

3. A leadership-releasing strategy

II. The Equipping of the Business Person

A. The church is responsible for equipping the business person. (Ephesians 4:11-12)

1. Equipping through strategic relationships

Empowering and Releasing the Business Person

> Generous giving is the result of an inspired motive.
> V.H. LEWIS

    2. Equipping through <u>strategic teaching classes</u>

    3. Equipping through <u>strategic retreats and materials</u>

B. The business person receiving equipping from other sources:

    1. The body of Christ has many great resources the businessperson should be aware of.

    2. The body of Christ has some strange, unbiblical and carnal manipulative teachings the businessperson should be aware of.

    3. The body of Christ has produced many books, magazines, seminars and conferences that may or may not be beneficial to the businessperson.

III. Releasing the Business Person for Fruitful Ministry

A. The business person has spiritual gifts:

    1. The gift of <u>leadership</u>

    2. The gift of <u>faith</u>

    3. The gift of <u>giving</u>

    4. The gift of <u>discernment</u>

    5. The gift of <u>administration</u>

    6. The gift of <u>teaching</u>

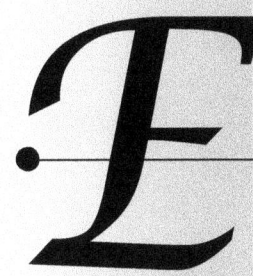

Empowering and Releasing the Business Person

    B.   The business person needs a place in the church to function.

        1.   The businessperson does not want to be looked upon by the pastor or church leadership as a potential money supplier only.

        2.   The businessperson does not want to be called upon to do all the tasks the pastor does not want to do – the administration, budgeting, etc. They want more than what they do every day on the job.

        3.   The businessperson has spiritual gifts that need to be recognized, nurtured and released into the local church and into the marketplace. Both are essential to true spiritual fulfillment.

IV. Receiving God's Blessing Upon Your Business

    A.   Blessing Scriptures

        1.   GENESIS 1:22, 28 "And God blessed them, saying, 'Be fruitful and multiply, and fill the waters in the seas, and let birds multiply on the earth.' … Then God blessed them, and God said to them, 'Be fruitful and multiply; fill the earth and subdue it; have dominion over the fish of the sea, over the birds of the air, and over every living thing that moves on the earth.'"

        2.   DEUTERONOMY 2:7 "For the Lord your God has blessed you in all the work of your hand. He knows your trudging through this great wilderness. These forty years the Lord your God has been with you; you have lacked nothing."

        3.   DEUTERONOMY 11:27 "The blessing, if you obey the commandments of the Lord your God which I command you today."

        4.   DEUTERONOMY 12:7 "And there you shall eat before the Lord your God, and you shall rejoice in all to which you have put your hand, you and your households, in which the Lord your God has blessed you."

        5.   DEUTERONOMY 28:3-6 "Blessed shall you be in the city, and blessed shall you be in the country. Blessed shall be the fruit of your body, the produce of your ground and the increase of your herds, the increase of your cattle and the offspring of your flocks. Blessed shall be your basket and your kneading bowl. Blessed shall you be when you come in, and blessed shall you be when you go out."

Empowering and Releasing the Business Person

6. DEUTERONOMY 29:9 "Therefore keep the words of this covenant, and do them, that you may prosper in all that you do."
7. JOSHUA 1:7-8 "Only be strong and very courageous, that you may observe to do according to all the law which Moses My servant commanded you; do not turn from it to the right hand or to the left, that you may prosper wherever you go. This Book of the Law shall not depart from your mouth, but you shall meditate in it day and night, that you may observe to do according to all that is written in it. For then you will make your way prosperous, and then you will have good success."
8. 2 SAMUEL 6:11-12 "The ark of the Lord remained in the house of Obed-Edom the Gittite three months. And the Lord blessed Obed-Edom and all his household. Now it was told King David, saying, 'The Lord has blessed the house of Obed-Edom and all that belongs to him, because of the ark of God.' So David went and brought up the ark of God from the house of Obed-Edom to the City of David with gladness."
9. 2 SAMUEL 7:29 "Now therefore, let it please You to bless the house of Your servant, that it may continue forever before You; for You, O Lord GOD, have spoken it, and with Your blessing let the house of Your servant be blessed forever."
10. 1 KINGS 2:3 "And keep the charge of the Lord your God: to walk in His ways, to keep His statutes, His commandments, His judgments, and His testimonies, as it is written in the Law of Moses, that you may prosper in all that you do and wherever you turn."
11. 2 CHRONICLES 26:5 "He (Uzziah) sought God in the days of Zechariah, who had understanding in the visions of God; and as long as he sought the Lord, God made him prosper."
12. 2 CHRONICLES 31:10 "And Azariah the chief priest, from the house of Zadok, answered him and said, 'Since the people began to bring the offerings into the house of the Lord, we have had enough to eat and have plenty left, for the Lord has blessed His people; and what is left is this great abundance.'"
13. PSALM 1:1-3 "Blessed is the man who walks not in the counsel of the ungodly, nor stands in the path of sinners, nor sits in the seat of the scornful; but his delight is in the law of the Lord, and in His law he meditates day and night. He shall be like a tree planted by the rivers of water, that brings forth its fruit in its season, whose leaf also shall not wither; and whatever he does shall prosper."
14. PSALM 32:1-2 "Blessed is he whose transgression is forgiven, whose sin is covered. Blessed is the man to whom the Lord does not impute iniquity, and in whose spirit there is no deceit."
15. PSALM 34:8 "Oh, taste and see that the Lord is good; blessed is the man who trusts in Him!"
16. PSALM 37:21 "The wicked borrows and does not repay, but the righteous shows mercy and gives."
17. PSALM 40:4 "Blessed is that man who makes the Lord his trust, and does not respect the proud, nor such as turn aside to lies."
18. PSALM 41:1-2 "Blessed is he who considers the poor; the Lord will deliver him in time of trouble. The Lord will preserve him and keep him alive, and he will be blessed on the earth; you will not deliver him to the will of his enemies."

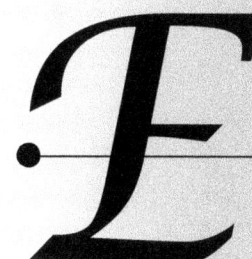# Empowering and Releasing the Business Person

19. PSALM 106:3 "Blessed are those who keep justice, and he who does righteousness at all times!"
20. PSALM 65:4 "Blessed is the man You choose, and cause to approach You, that he may dwell in Your courts. We shall be satisfied with the goodness of Your house, of Your holy temple."
21. PSALM 84:4-5,12 "Blessed are those who dwell in Your house; they will still be praising You. Blessed is the man whose strength is in You, whose heart is set on pilgrimage… O Lord of hosts, blessed is the man who trusts in You!"
22. PSALM 94:12 "Blessed is the man whom You instruct, O Lord, and teach out of Your law."
23. PSALM 112:1-2 "Praise the Lord! Blessed is the man who fears the Lord, who delights greatly in His commandments. His descendants will be mighty on earth; the generation of the upright will be blessed."
24. PSALM 118:26 "Blessed is he who comes in the name of the Lord! We have blessed you from the house of the Lord."
25. PSALM 119:1-2 "Blessed are the undefiled in the way, who walk in the law of the Lord! Blessed are those who keep His testimonies, who seek Him with the whole heart!"
26. PSALM 128:1,4 "Blessed is every one who fears the Lord, who walks in His ways… Behold, thus shall the man be blessed who fears the Lord."
27. PROVERBS 8:34 "Blessed is the man who listens to me, watching daily at my gates, waiting at the posts of my doors."
28. PROVERBS 10:22 "The blessing of the Lord makes one rich, and He adds no sorrow with it."
29. PROVERBS 11:27 "He who earnestly seeks good finds favor, but trouble will come to him who seeks evil."
30. PROVERBS 12:2 "A good man obtains favor from the Lord, but a man of wicked intentions He will condemn."
31. PROVERBS 22:9 "He who has a generous eye will be blessed, for he gives of his bread to the poor."
32. 1 CORINTHIANS 16:2 "On the first day of the week let each one of you lay something aside, storing up as he may prosper, that there be no collections when I come."
33. 2 CORINTHIANS 9:5-6 "Therefore I thought it necessary to exhort the brethren to go to you ahead of time, and prepare your generous gift beforehand, which you had previously promised, that it may be ready as a matter of generosity and not as a grudging obligation. But this I say: He who sows sparingly will also reap sparingly, and he who sows bountifully will also reap bountifully."
34. EPHESIANS 1:3 "Blessed be the God and Father of our Lord Jesus Christ, who has blessed us with every spiritual blessing in the heavenly places in Christ."
35. HEBREWS 6:7 "For the earth which drinks in the rain that often comes upon it, and bears herbs useful for those by whom it is cultivated, receives blessing from God."
36. 3 JOHN 1:2 "Beloved, I pray that you may prosper in all things and be in health, just as your soul prospers."

Empowering and Releasing the Business Person

B. The Blessed Business

Business God's Way → Blessing Obtained

7. Faith attitude
6. Diligence
5. Wisdom
4. Humility
3. Healthy relationships
2. Unquestionable integrity
1. Kingdom focus

Business Man's Way → Blessing Hindered

1. Faulty ambition
2. Blind ambition
3. Enough is never enough
4. Imbalanced priorities
5. Manipulation of people
6. Pride
7. Laziness

Empowering and Releasing the Business Person

Empowering People for Supernatural Provision

Session #5

> Empowering the people you lead to believe for and reach out to receive supernatural provision is of utmost importance. God may use the practical and tangible means to provide for His people through their jobs, investments, and immediate world of opportunities, or He may choose to provide supernaturally using the realm of miracles. The supernatural is when God provides for His people outside of their normal world of living, outside of what is already in their hands or in their bank account. The leader must lead the people to the edge of faith, pushing people out of the limitation boxes, pushing people out of only what the natural mind can conceive. We must teach people to become willing channels by which God's abundant blessings flow. This channel may be narrow and shallow at first, yet in time the waters of God's abundance will flow freely. If we, by faith, yield ourselves, the channel becomes wider and wider, deeper and deeper, allowing a supernatural abundant to flow through us.

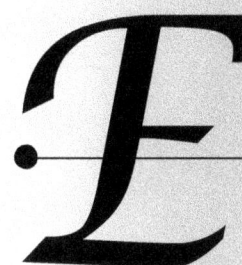

Empowering People for Supernatural Provision

Supernatural Provision Scriptures

GENESIS 22:8
And Abraham said, "My son, God will provide for Himself the lamb for a burnt offering."

GENESIS 22:14
And Abraham called the name of the place, The-Lord-Will-Provide; as it is said to this day, "In the Mount of The Lord it shall be provided."

GENESIS 45:11
There I will provide for you, lest you and your household, and all that you have, come to poverty; for there are still five years of famine.

ISAIAH 45:3
I will give you the treasures of darkness and hidden riches of secret places, that you may know that I, the Lord, who call you by your name, am the God of Israel.

DEUTERONOMY 2:7
For the Lord your God has blessed you in all the work of your hand. He knows your trudging through this great wilderness. These forty years the Lord your God has been with you; you have lacked nothing.

NEHEMIAH 9:21
Forty years You sustained them in the wilderness, they lacked nothing; their clothes did not wear out and their feet did not swell.

PHILIPPIANS 4:19
And my God shall supply all your need according to His riches in glory by Christ Jesus.

EXODUS 16:4
Then the Lord said to Moses, "Behold, I will rain bread from heaven for you. And the people shall go out and gather a certain quota every day, that I may test them, whether they will walk in My law or not."

EXODUS 17:6
Behold, I will stand before you there on the rock in Horeb; and you shall strike the rock, and water will come out of it, that the people may drink.

DEUTERONOMY 30:9
The Lord your God will make you abound in all the work of your hand, in the fruit of your body, in the increase of your livestock, and in the produce of your land for good. For the Lord will again rejoice over you for good as He rejoiced over your fathers,

MATTHEW 17:27
…Go to the sea, cast in a hook, and take the fish that comes up first. And when you have opened its mouth, you will find a piece of money; take that and give it to them for Me and you.

MATTHEW 14:19-21
And He took the five loaves and the two fish, and looking up to heaven, He blessed and broke and gave the loaves to the disciples; and the disciples gave to the multitudes. So they all ate and were filled, and they took up twelve baskets full of the fragments that remained. Now those who had eaten were about five thousand men, besides women and children.

Empowering People for Supernatural Provision

I. The National Spiritual Crisis and Economical Connection

(1 Kings 16:29-34)

> When we are deprived for a time of the most ordinary blessings of life, then do we become vividly conscious of their former presence and their unspeakable value.

A. The Nation's <u>Leadership Backslidden</u>
(1 Kings 16:29-30)

B. The Nation <u>Worshipped Idols</u>
(1 Kings 16:32-33)

C. The Nation <u>Provoked God to Anger</u>
(1 Kings 16:33)

D. The Nation <u>in Economic Crisis</u>
(Deuteronomy 26:18; 1 Kings 17:1)

II. The Natural World Used for Supernatural Provision

(1 Kings 17:2-7)

> God uses the natural realm to provide supernaturally.

A. The Natural World God Uses
(Ruth 2:12; Proverbs 10:4; 12:24; 31:20)

1. Your <u>life</u>
2. Your <u>job</u>
3. Your <u>business</u>
4. Your <u>world</u>
5. Your <u>friends</u>
6. Your <u>family</u>
7. Your <u>government</u>

> The greatest blessings are apt to be regarded with indifference because of the constancy of their supply.

For over 60 years, Oseola McCarty of Hattiesburg, Mississippi, washed other people's clothes using only a large pot and a scrub board and never revealing a secret. There was good money in washing clothes, and she was saving half of it. She began saving pennies and nickels, and when McCarty retired very comfortably at the age of 87, she was able to establish a $150,000 to a scholarship fund at the University of Southern Mississippi.[1]

---

[1] Kevin Chappell, "The Washerwoman Philanthropist" <u>Ebony magazine</u>, (Johnson Publishing Company, Inc., 1995).

Empowering People for Supernatural Provision

    B.   The Natural Things Become Starting Points for Miracles

        1.   What's in <u>your hand</u>?
            (Exodus 4:1-2; Deuteronomy 30:9; Proverbs 3:27; Eccl 9:10)

        2.   What's in <u>your house</u>?
            (1 Kings 17:8-16; Psalm 112:3)

        3.   What's in <u>your basket</u>?
            (John 6:11-13)

        4.   What's in <u>your mind</u>?
            (Psalm 24:4; Philippians 4:19; Proverbs 12:5; Isaiah 55:8;
            Jeremiah 29:1; Isaiah 45:3)

III. The Instruments of Supernatural Provision

(1 Kings 17:4-6)

    A.   The Surprise of Supernatural Provision Changing
        (1 Kings 17:7)

    "After awhile the brook dried up"

        1.   Dried up brooks of the <u>unemployed</u>.

        2.   Dried up brooks of the <u>investment nightmare</u>.

        3.   Dried up brooks of <u>bankruptcy</u>.

        4.   Dried up brooks of <u>investment easy business success</u>.

    B.   The Surprising Providers God Uses
        (1 Kings 17:6)

        1.   The unlikely provider of the <u>dirty birds</u>
            (1 Kings 17:6)

        2.   The unlikely provider of the <u>four lepers</u>
            (2 Kings 7:3-8)

        3.   The unlikely provider of the <u>fish</u> (Matthew 17:27)

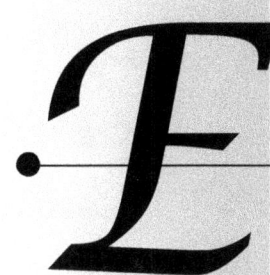

Empowering People for Supernatural Provision

IV. Lessons Learned In The School Of Supernatural Provision

A. We learn the lesson that God has control over all supply and honors those who honor His word.
(Joshua 24:13; Psalm 24:1; Deuteronomy 28:13; Joshua 1:8)

B. We learn the lesson that a bad national economy does not affect God's ability to provide for us supernaturally.
(Psalm 112:3; Isaiah 30:23)

C. We learn the lesson that God can use abandoned and godless means and people to supply for us in a time of need.
(Proverbs 13:22; Ecclesiastes 2:26; Philippians 4:19)

D. We learn the lesson that God frequently does not make known His supernatural provision until the need is pressing us beyond what we can do.
(Exodus 14:16)

E. We learn the lesson that "scarcity thinking" is different than true scarcity, and the spirit of poverty is different than poverty itself.
(Romans 8:15-17; Luke 6:38; Matthew 25:29)

F. We learn the lesson that God's supernatural provision is found in hearing and obeying God's voice.
(Deuteronomy 5:32; Job 23:12; Job 36:11)

G. We learn the lesson that God's abundant supply may come from unexpected sources at unexpected times.
(Matthew 17:27; John 6:11-12)

H. We can learn the lesson that God's supernatural provision can be released by sacrificial giving out of our need.
(1 Kings 17:8-16; Luke 4:24-27)

Empowering People for Supernatural Provision

Empowering The Giving Of Your Church
Giving, Receiving and Prospering

Giving, Receiving and Prospering

Sermon #1

Giving, Receiving, Prospering
Learning to Live the Truth That Activates Financial Blessing

Part 3: Growing in the Grace of Giving

II Corinthians 8:7; II Chronicles 16:9; Luke 6:38; Romans 12:6; Malachi 3:8-10

INTRODUCTION As a local church pastor, I have a deep desire to bring God's people into greater blessings. I am committed to Christ and to the Holy Spirit to proclaim all the truth of scripture. This, of course, includes God's thinking in our finances. Essentially what we seek is to come into greater realization of the Lordship of Jesus Christ over our entire life, including our material possessions. We have laid a strong foundation in our first two messages on giving our tithe and receiving the blessings that belong to us. We shall now develop the truth of giving not only our tithes, but our offerings. This is a voluntary, free-will giving that becomes a matter of faith, vision and grace.

GIVING	*"Honor the Lord with your substance and with the firstfruits of all your increase" Pr 3:9* Giving activates divine law that releases the work of God in our private world.
RECEIVING	*"So your barns will be filled with plenty" (Pr 3:10a)* God responds to our giving by opening up opportunities to receive divine provisions both directly and indirectly from His hand
PROSPERING	*"And your vats will overflow with new wine" 3:10b* God desires that we receive abundantly and have more than enough so as to become a liberal giver.
LIFESTYLE STEWARDSHIP	*Luke 16:13 "No servant can serve two masters; for either he will hate the one and love the other, or else he will be loyal to the one and despise the other. You cannot serve God and mammon."* A steward is a guardian of the interests of another. The steward owns nothing, but is careful to guard, protect and increase the property of the one whom he serves. We are stewards of time, strength, ability as well as our money.

GIVING OUR TITHE

- Tithing is the first of our wages and the first of our increase.
- Tithing is the acknowledgement that all we have belongs to the Lord.
- Tithe is to be given with an attitude of worship.
- Tithing is the sacred portion we set aside as the Lord's.
- Tithe is not to be used for our personal needs.
- Tithe is to be given as an act of spiritual obedience.
- Tithing is not just Old Testament teaching; both Jesus and the apostles confirmed tithing.
- Tithe is to be given willingly with a joyful heart of expectation.
- Tithing is the biblical minimum and will not limit our giving but will open the door to a genuine stewardship.
- Tithing is a token of consecration that one has surrendered all and made Him Lord.
- Tithe is to be brought faithfully into the storehouse, which is the local church.
- Tithing is an adventure in blessing, an opportunity to prove God.
- Tithing opens the windows of heaven for God to pour out a personalized, custom-made blessing.
- Tithing prepares for an enlarging of your capacity for the blessings of God.
- Tithing is aligning yourself with the authority of God to rebuke the devourer.
- Tithing is putting my trust in God's ability to take care of me and His desire to remove the curse from my finance.

I. THE GIVING OF VOLUNTARY OFFERINGS
(Malachi 3:8; 2 Corinthians 9:7)

    A. The Difference Between Tithes and Offerings

        1. Tithe = Webster dictionary defines tithe as the tenth part of anything. Tithe is the firstfruits of all we earn and already belongs to the Lord. It is our minimum financial commitment.

        2. Offerings = An offering is an undesignated amount given as a freewill love gift unto the Lord. We are encouraged in the scriptures to grow in giving of offerings. This is where liberality and generosity are matured.

    B. The Heart Attitude of Freewill Offerings
(Ezra 1:4; 3:5; 7:16; Psalm 96:8)

        1. Willing Heart
(Exodus 25:2; 35:5,21-22)

        2. Stirred Heart
(Exodus 35:21)

3. Sacrificial Heart
(Exodus 35:22-29)

4. Loyal Heart
(1 Chronicles 29:3)

5. Rejoicing Heart
(1 Chronicles 29:9)

II. PROFILE OF TRUE GIVERS

A. True Givers desire to give their best to forward God's work.
(Genesis 22:2-8; 22;13; 4:3-5; Romans 12:1-2)

B. True Givers are motivated by grace, not guilt, competition or pressure.
(2 Corinthians 8:1; 9:7-8; Romans 12:6; Proverbs 22:9)

1. II Corinthians 8:1 "I desire brethren to make known to you the <u>manifestation</u> of <u>God's grace</u> which has been given in the churches of Macedonia."
   - Godspeed: "I must tell you brothers, how the favor of God has been shown in the churches of Macedonia."
   - Beck: "Fellow Christians, we want you to know what God's gift of love has done in the churches of Macedonia."
   - NIV: "And now, brothers, we want you to know about the grace that God has given the Macedonian churches."

   a. Macedonian churches: Philippi, Thessalonica, Berea, these were churches that had experienced natural catastrophe. An earthquake destroyed cities, ruined their economy and were in great tribulation.
   b. Divine Enablement: God will enable you to give strength to you
   c. Divine Generosity: God will put generosity into your heart

2. Grace Defined
   a. *Charis*, found ten times in II Corinthians 8-9, referring either to the divine generosity favorably displayed or to divine enablement to participate worthily in the collection.
   b. Act of grace, offering denoting the act of giving itself
   c. Grace: that which bestows or occasions pleasure, delight or causes favorable regard, to be joyful, mercy. To dignify or raise by an act of favor, to honor, to bless, lift up, to supply with all that is needed.

3. Grace: our motivator/stimulator for giving
   a. It's grace that motivates us to give; grace initiates giving.
   b. It's grace—not law, not rules, not guilt, not competition—that stimulates a Christian to give.
   c. It's grace that gives us the ability to give, the desire to give, motivates us to move into faith.

C. True Givers give sacrificially not just out of surplus.
   (2 Corinthians 8:2-3; Mark 12:42-43; 2 Samuel 24:24)

   1. II Cor 8:2 "How that in a great trial of affliction the abundance of their joy and their deep poverty abounded unto the riches of their liberality."
      a. CON: "For in the heavy trial which has proved their steadfastness, the fullness of their joy has overflowed out of the depth of their poverty in the richness of their liberality."
      b. NEB: "The troubles they have been through have tried them hard, yet in all this they have been so exuberantly happy that from the depths of their poverty they have shown themselves lavishly open-handed!"
      c. LENSKI: "That in a great test of affliction the excess of their joy and their down to depth poverty exceeded in the riches of their single-mindedness."

   2. Examples of those who gave out of poverty: The poor widow's mite (Mark 12:41-44)
      a. RSV: "But she out of her poverty has put in everything she had, her whole living."
      b. WEY: "But she out of her need has thrown in all she possessed, all she had to live on."
      c. KNOX: "She with so little to give, put in all that she had, her whole livelihood."

   3. II Corinthians 8:3 "For I testify that according to their ability and beyond their ability they gave of their own accord."
      a. CON: "They have given not only according to their means but beyond their means and that of their own free will."
      b. BAS: For I give them witness, that as they were able, and even more than they were able, they gave from the impulse of their hearts.
      c. KNOX: They undertook to do all they could and more than they could.
      d. PHILLIPS: "...I can guarantee that they were willing to give to the limit of their means, yes and beyond their means, without the slightest urging from me or anyone else."

  e. LENSKI: "Despite their deep poverty, they insisted on giving far more than anyone could ever think they could give, they made a joy of robbing themselves."

  f. EXPOSITOR'S BIBLE: "They gave far more generously than their slender means and adverse circumstances really permitted them. Not that their judgement was imbalanced but their eagerness to contribute led them to surpass all expectations!"

D. True Givers give in faith recognizing the laws of harvest.
(2 Corinthians 9:6; Proverbs 11:24-26; Genesis 8:22; Psalm 126:6; Galatians 6:9; Hebrews 11:6; Matthew 17:20; Luke 6:38)

III. A Model Prayer For True Givers

I Chronicles 29:10-15

Therefore David blessed the Lord before all the assembly; and David said: "Blessed are You, Lord God of Israel, our Father, forever and ever. Yours, O Lord, is the greatness, the power and the glory, the victory and the majesty; for all that is in heaven and in earth is Yours; yours is the kingdom, O Lord, and You are exalted as head over all. Both riches and honor come from You, and You reign over all. In Your hand is power and might; in Your hand it is to make great and to give strength to all. "Now therefore, our God, we thank You and praise Your glorious name. But who am I, and who are my people, that we should be able to offer so willingly as this? For all things come from You, and of Your own we have given You. For we are aliens and pilgrims before You, as were all our fathers; our days on earth are as a shadow, and without hope.

Our Acknowledgements:

We acknowledge His supreme dominion and universal authority

We acknowledge our total dependence on God

We acknowledge His ownership and our stewardship

We acknowledge our life here as a sojourner

Slide #1

Giving
Receiving
Prospering

Learning to Live the Truth That Activates Financial Blessing

Slide #2

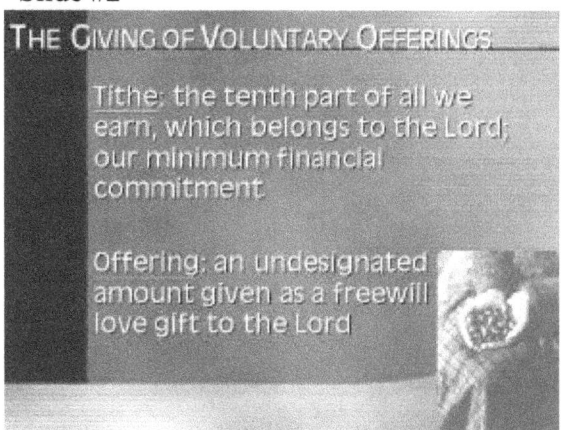

THE GIVING OF VOLUNTARY OFFERINGS

Tithe: the tenth part of all we earn, which belongs to the Lord; our minimum financial commitment

Offering: an undesignated amount given as a freewill love gift to the Lord

Slide #3

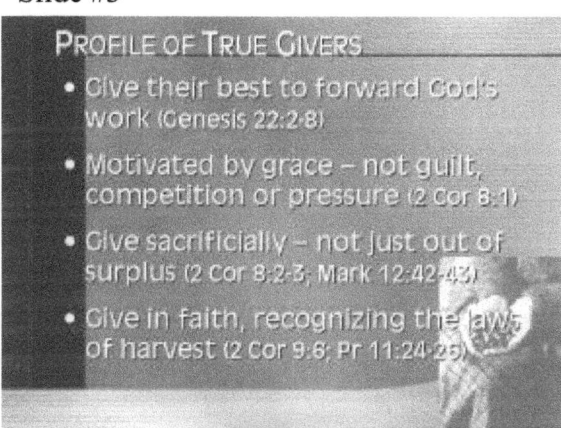

PROFILE OF TRUE GIVERS

- Give their best to forward God's work (Genesis 22:2-8)
- Motivated by grace – not guilt, competition or pressure (2 Cor 8:1)
- Give sacrificially – not just out of surplus (2 Cor 8:2-3; Mark 12:42-43)
- Give in faith, recognizing the laws of harvest (2 Cor 9:6; Pr 11:24-25)

Slide #4

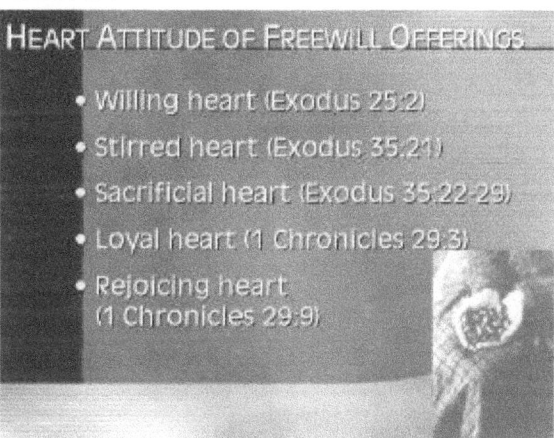

HEART ATTITUDE OF FREEWILL OFFERINGS

- Willing heart (Exodus 25:2)
- Stirred heart (Exodus 35:21)
- Sacrificial heart (Exodus 35:22-29)
- Loyal heart (1 Chronicles 29:3)
- Rejoicing heart (1 Chronicles 29:9)

Slide #5

MODEL PRAYER FOR TRUE GIVERS
1 Chronicles 29:10-15

- We acknowledge God's supreme dominion and universal authority
- We acknowledge our total dependence on God
- We acknowledge His ownership and our stewardship
- We acknowledge our life here as a sojourner

Giving a Faith Harvest Offering

Sermon #2

Giving a Faith Harvest Offering
A Faith Harvest Congregational Attitude

1 Chronicles 29:2-5, 14-18

INTRODUCTION: Giving of our finance is a spiritual matter. It involves the heart, our spiritual capacity for faith in God and His invisible powers. Giving reflects our value system, our life priorities and our life discipline. Seeing God work in our material world of things will enlarge our faith for the invisible world of the kingdom of God. As the senior pastor of City Bible Church, I have sought to establish a clear biblical foundation for the giving of our finance. There are more than one thousand references to money in the Bible.

The scripture clearly teaches specific kinds of giving: the giving of our tithe and the giving of our offerings. If you are not handling your finances in line with God's plan, then your whole life may be out of joint. No matter how spiritual you are in other areas, you will never know the real blessing and reign of God in your life until you bring your money in line with the will of God as revealed in His word. The Bible clearly reveals that God does have a plan for our money. Certainly the things we accumulate are not important. They are simply tools for us in accomplishing God's work.

"The U.S. Department of Commerce has recently released statistics on American churches, clergy and church schools. Church Law & Tax Report gave some interesting figures: Of special interest are the statistics on who is supporting these churches. Persons 65-74 years of age donated the largest percentage of their income (3.1 percent) and those 18-24 the least (0.6 percent). Increasingly, those with lower incomes gave a higher proportion of their income to charity than higher income individuals. Persons with household incomes of under $10,000 gave 2.8 percent of their total incomes, while those with incomes over $100,000 gave only 2.1 percent. The average annual contribution to the church was $715 per household."[1] Giving should be an outward, material expression of a deep spiritual commitment, an indication of a willing and obedient heart. Today we are addressing the subject of faith harvest giving, a special, once a year commitment toward a special one-time offering. This is a special love gift, a seed gift as we view our future year. We begin our faith harvest giving, above our tithe, this weekend and we will continue to present it to the Lord until January 24.

I. FAITH TO BE A GREAT STEWARD

    A. Stewardship Lifestyle: A steward is a guardian of the interests of another. The steward owns nothing, but is careful to guard, protect and increase the property of the one whom he serves. We are stewards of time, strength, ability as well as our money. (Luke 16:1-13)
- "Stewardship is an act of worship, thus we should recognize that God is the owner of all things and all we do should be done by keeping His objectives, best interests and glorification in mind."

- J.L. Kraft, head of the Kraft Cheese Corporation, who had given approximately 25% of his enormous income to Christian causes for many years, said, "The only investment I ever made which has paid consistently increasing dividends is the money I have given to the Lord."[2]

    B.   Stewardship Three-Step Plan

> "Give according to your income, lest God make your income like your giving."
>
> "God's bank remains open regardless of the circumstances."
>
> "You will reap more than you sow; God will return to you in multiplied form."

        1.   Giving: Giving activates divine law that releases the work of God in our private world.
(Proverbs 3:9)

            a.   Giving of our tithe: our firstfruits, our first part, ten percent first. The foundation to your stewardship plan is a dedicated tithe, now, today. God has asked for our tithe, the first and best of all that we receive. That means we should tithe from our total income. Any profit made from the sale of a home ought to be tithed upon because it is in fact part of our first fruits. Inheritances, insurance monies, dividends, interest, these are all parts of our increase. A farmer first sets aside a portion from the harvest for seed to plant the following year. If he didn't, he wouldn't have another crop.
(Ezekiel 44:30)

            b.   Giving our offerings: an offering is a free-will unlimited amount given by the giver with faith and joy.

        2.   Receiving: God responds to our giving by opening up opportunities to receive divine provisions both directly and indirectly from His hand
(Proverbs 3:10; Luke 6:38)

        3.   Prospering: God desires that we receive abundantly and have more than enough to become a liberal giver.
(Proverbs 3:10)

II. Giving A Faith Harvest Offering

A faith harvest offering is given by the believer with the knowledge that this seed is sowed in faith, believing God to water it and enable it to become the full harvest of what God desires to bring into my life. This is a faith offering, a specific giving with liberality and sacrifice.

    A.   A faith harvest offering is given out of a willing heart
(Ezra 1:4; Ezra 7:16; Psalm 96:8; Exodus 25:2; 35:5)

B. A faith harvest offering is given out of a stirring of the Holy Spirit.
(Exodus 35:21)

    1. Giving faith offerings is an individual event. You must be stirred yourself.

    2. Our outlook is too small, but that smallness can be shaken off in answer to our Lord who has called us to be big people.

    3. Stirred to become big in our world view, big in our love for the lost, big in our giving.

C. A faith harvest offering is given out of my own special treasure.
(1 Chronicles 29:3)

    1. Give out of what I have and could have if I am willing to sell something, do without something. Give over something precious. Kids, sell a toy or give up a special toy. Children: give up money from a Christmas gift.

    2. The fear of losing what I have blocks the door to what I can become. Turn everything over the Lord. Learn to give as you have been given to and discover the unlimited possibilities God can give to you. He is a God of resource and fullness.

D. A faith harvest offering is a sacrificial offering.
(2 Samuel 24:24; Mark 12:41-44; 2 Corinthians 8:3)

    1. Start with a sacrifice of something in your hands; a precious gift is one that means something to you.
(2 Corinthians 8:2)

    2. Examples of those who gave out of poverty: The poor widow's mite
(Mark 12:42-43)

    3. Give according to and beyond your ability, of your own accord.
(2 Corinthians 8:3)

E. A faith harvest offering is motivated by grace not guilt, competition or pressure.
(2 Corinthians 8:1; 9:7-8)

    1. 2 Corinthians 8:1 "I desire brethren to make known to you the <u>manifestation</u> of <u>God's grace</u> which has been given in the churches of Macedonia.

2. Grace is:
   a. ***Divine Enablement***: God will enable you to give strength to you
   b. ***Divine Generosity***: God will put generosity into your heart
   c. ***Divine Willingness***: God will prompt you, quicken you, make you ready to act.
   d. ***Divine Motivation***: God will give us the ability to give and the desire to give.

F. A faith harvest offering is a seed faith offering, planting for the future.
(2 Corinthians 9:6; Genesis 8:22; Psalm 126:6; Galatians 6:9; Matthew 17:20; Proverbs 11:24-26; 2 Cor 9:10-11)
- NAS: Now this {I say,} he who sows sparingly shall also reap sparingly; and he who sows bountifully shall also reap bountifully.
- NIV: Remember this: Whoever sows sparingly will also reap sparingly, and whoever sows generously will also reap generously.
- Trent: "Remember the saying, scanty sowing, scanty harvest, plentiful sowing, plentiful harvest."
- Moffat: "He who sows generously will reap a generous harvest."
- Lenski: "Now this, he who keeps sowing sparingly, sparingly shall he also reap, and he who keeps sowing on the basis of blessings, on the basis of blessings shall he also reap.
- Lit Con: "This to, be ready thus, as a bounty and not as greed; who is sowing sparingly, sparingly shall be reaping also, and who is sowing bountifully, bountifully shall be reaping also, each according as he has proposed."
- Gr: "He who sows on the basis or principle of blessing, he shall reap on this basis and the principle."

1. Seed must be planted. Giving is the seeding for our miracle from which God our source will multiply.

2. Move beyond what is in your hand and believe for the blessing of God upon your future. How big of a field do you see? Your dream, your vision, your job, your business, your world. How much faith do you have in that seed to grow?

3. I will plant my seed. God will move my mountain!

4. When a farmer scatters seeds, it looks like he is wasting seed, just throwing handfuls everywhere. But the more seed he throws, the more harvest he reaps. We must see the same principle operated in the <u>financial</u> realm that God has established in the <u>farming</u> realm. Just as a farmer depends upon the blessing the Creator puts on his "invested seed," he trusts the same Creator to take the financial seed invested when we give, no matter how little, and multiply it.

III. Conclusion

    A.   I would like the entire congregation to take the Faith Harvest card in your hand and kneel before the Lord. We will pray now together for the Holy Spirit to speak clearly this year as we give in faith, with sacrifice and with joy.

    B.   A faith promise pledge is what I am believing God to allow me to give according to His gracious provision in my life. This is not a budgetary decision only. It is not based on what I can do. It is a faith-releasing promise, based on my prayerful seeking of the Lord. We are praying for God to release through us His gifts of divine provision.

    C.   I would like all the elders and district pastors to come first and pray for the seed that my wife and I are sowing. Then I will pray for their seed. Then the lay pastors are to come and have the elders pray over their faith-seed. Then the whole church will come.

Faith harvest money is given as a faith offering. This money is used as God enables the eldership to see needs outside our church and special needs inside our church that cannot be met by our normal set budget. We then sow the money into fertile ministry fields. Last year we were able to help with the following:
- Helping city pastors in crisis, city pastors monthly meetings and city pastors breakfasts
- Bible college scholarships for international students
- Christian education programs
- Church planting
- Missions: Laos, South Africa, Romania, Uganda, Mexico, Bolivia, , Russia, Cambodia, Malaysia, Pakistan
- Laotian outreach every Sunday night
- Portland public school outreach
- Remodeling/landscaping of church grounds
- City summer celebration
- ESL outreach
- Eternity drama (18,000 people came to see it; 860 made public confessions to accept Christ)
- Outreach churches in crises or in building programs we seed into their field
- Children's evangelistic outreach
- City outreach food house
- We have used faith harvest to launch CBC evangelistic ministries and other ministries that otherwise would not exist without the faith harvest giving

---

[1] *Pulpit Helps*, August, 1992, p. 8. Sermonillustrations.com November 10, 2001.
[2] W. A. Criswell, <u>A Guidebook for Pastors</u>, p. 154. Esermons.com

Slide #1

Giving a Faith Harvest Offering

Slide #2

1 CHRONICLES 29:2-5
Now for the house of my God I have prepared with all my might: gold for things to be made of gold, silver for things of silver, bronze for things of bronze, iron for things of iron, wood for things of wood, onyx stones, stones to be set, glistening stones of various colors, all kinds of precious stones, and marble slabs in abundance.

Slide #3

Moreover, because I have set my affection on the house of my God, I have given to the house of my God, over and above all that I have prepared for the holy house, my own special treasure of gold and silver: three thousand talents of gold, of the gold of Ophir, and seven thousand talents of refined silver, to overlay the walls of the houses; the gold for things of gold and the silver for things of silver, and for all kinds of work to be done by the hands of craftsmen. Who then is willing to consecrate himself this day to the Lord?"

Slide #4

1 CHRONICLES 29:14-16
But who am I, and who are my people, that we should be able to offer so willingly as this? For all things come from You, and of Your own we have given You. For we are aliens and pilgrims before You, as were all our fathers; Our days on earth are as a shadow, and without hope. O Lord our God, all this abundance that we have prepared to build You a house for Your holy name is from Your hand, and is all Your own.

Slide #5

I know also, my God, that You test the heart and have pleasure in uprightness. As for me, in the uprightness of my heart I have willingly offered all these things; and now with joy I have seen Your people, who are present here to offer willingly to You. O Lord God of Abraham, Isaac, and Israel, our fathers, keep this forever in the intent of the thoughts of the heart of Your people, and fix their heart toward You.

Slide #6

Faith to be a Great Steward

We are stewards of our time, strength, ability, and money.

A steward is a guardian of the interests of another. The steward owns nothing, but is careful to guard, protect and increase the property of the one he serves.

Slide #7

The Stewardship Three-Step Plan

1. **Giving**: Giving activates divine law that releases the work of God in our private world (Pr 3:9).
2. **Receiving**: God responds to our giving by opening up opportunities to receive divine provision both directly and indirectly from His hand (Proverbs 3:10).
3. **Prospering**: God desires that we receive abundantly and have more than enough to become liberal givers (Pr 3:10).

Slide #8

Giving a Faith Harvest Offering

1. Given out of a willing heart (Ezra 1:4)
2. Given out of a stirring of the Holy Spirit (Ex 35:21)
3. Given out of a stirring of my own special treasure (1 Chron 29:3)
4. Given out of a stirring of a sacrificial offering (2 Sam 24:24)
5. Motivated by grace not guilt, competition or pressure (2 Cor 8:1)
6. A seed faith offering, planting for the future (2 Corinthians 9:6)

Empowering The Giving Of Your Church
Biblical Money Management

BIBLICAL MONEY MANAGEMENT

SERMON #3

Biblical Money Management
Applying Proven Biblical Principles to Manage and Increase Your Finances

- *Biblical money management is a discipline that touches every area of my life and requires a constant focus.*

  Three Types of Money Problems:
  1. You have a desire to give but have nothing to give – Money Problem
  2. You have a desire to give but have tied up your resources and can't give – Management Problem
  3. You have no desire to give, no desire for biblical management for any part of your life – Heart Problem

- *Biblical money management is the result of life management required of those who know Christ as savior and Lord.*
  (Acts 2;36; Acts 16:31; Romans 10:9)

- *Accepting Jesus Christ as Savior and not yielding to Him as Lord is incomplete acceptance.*

  A Call to Salvation is a Call to:
  1. Accept Jesus as Savior
  2. Submit to Him as your Lord
  3. Become a disciple: a disciplined follower of the Lord Jesus Christ

A.T. Tozer: "The Lord will not save those whom He cannot command. He will not divide His offices. You cannot believe on a half Christ. We take Him for what He is, the anointed Savior and Lord who is King of Kings and Lord of Lords. He would not be who He is if He saved us and called us and chose us without the understanding that He can also guide and control our lives."[1]

INTRODUCTION: God has called all believers to be good stewards. "…Give an account of your stewardship for you can no longer be a steward." Like the sirens sweet songs that lured Greek sailors to wreck their ships upon the rocks, the sweet of allure of financial gain and financial freedom causes many to shipwreck. True financial freedom comes when I use my money to acquire freedom for others instead of increasing my lifestyle pleasures. When is the best time to set our life in order, to manage what we have, and to become successful God's way and enjoy it? The best time to plant an oak tree is twenty years ago. The next best time is now! Even so for our finances, the best time was yesterday. The next best time is today, now! Do away with our somedays: Someday I'm going to. Someday after the next raise on my check. Someday when my ship comes. The illusive "someday" must be traded in for "today." The Matthew 25 parable paints a picture of stewardship. Out of three stewards, two were good and one was a failure. The poor steward hid his money in a hole in the ground. He mismanaged what he was given. God will take it away if we mismanage and He will reward us for proper management.

I. Purpose of This Series

A. Encourage every person toward a biblical perspective on managing their money properly and wisely.
(Matthew 6:19-21; 6:24; 6:31; Proverbs 24:3-4; Psalm 49:16-17; 62:10; Ecclesiastes 10:19)

B. Expose money problems as indicators that some things are out of order and that spiritual and biblical principles are being violated.
(Proverbs 12:1; 12:15; 12:25; 14:12; 15:19; 22:5)

   1. Even if we give to God our money, we cannot expect a miracle return if we are not managing what we have. There are spiritual and biblical reasons for money problems. We may be managing contrary to God's standards.

   2. Research shows that 85% of couples who divorce within the first five years said their number one source of their problem was conflict over money – how to save it, how to spend it, who gets what to do how much, how much debt they should carry, both having credit cards. They simply did not know how to handle their finances properly. They got themselves into deep financial bondage and, as a result, lost their love and respect for one another.

C. Encourage honest evaluation of life habits and bring about a change of mind and heart in the way we think about and use money.
(Proverbs 13:18; 28:6; 2 Corinthians 8:7)

D. Encourage every person to fast and pray about being a good steward, a manager of life and resources. The Holy Spirit desires to help us and will give us spiritual insights about money.
(1 Corinthians 2:12-13)

E. Encourage a liberal spirit of giving with a spirit of faith and expectation for your personal life, your family and the generation to come.
(Proverbs 11:24; Luke 6:38; 1 Timothy 6:18-19)

F. Encourage parents to teach their children through example and instruction how to live according to biblical values and priorities.

   1. Frustrated father talking with teenage son about money: "Son, just because you have checks in your checkbook doesn't mean you have money in your bank account."

2. Nationwide survey for high school seniors to research the financial IQ of teenagers. The findings of the research are as follows: Our high school seniors are financially illiterate. Basically teenagers know nothing about the basics of money, budgeting, value of a dollar, saving, and spending. All of these make no sense to the teenager.

3. Maybe we adults aren't doing that well ourselves with money management, both personally and nationally, seeing that our federal debt is 6.25 trillion. What does a trillion look like? If you had a tightly packed stack of $1,000 bills, one million would make a 4 inch stack, one billion a 300 foot stack (the length of a football field), one trillion would make a stack of 63 miles into the sky. Multiply that by 6.25 and that's our debt. (394 miles; stretch from Wilsonville, OR to Seattle, WA and back)

II. Biblical Money Management Principles We Will Learn

A. God has given us our life, our health, our talents and allowed us to work and receive money and possessions. It all comes from God's goodness.

B. God desires to bless us but requires us to manage wisely what we already have, living and spending money according to biblical values and principles.

C. God can bring prosperity into our life, give us more than enough and allow us to receive abundance of money knowing we have learned the purpose of prosperity.
(Deuteronomy 8:13-17)

---

[1] A. W. Tozer, *I Call It Heresy* (Camp Hill: Christian Publications, 1974), pp. 9, 14-16. 18-20.

Slide #1

Biblical Money Management

Applying Proven Biblical Principles to Manage and Increase Your Finances

Slide #2

Biblical money management is a discipline that touches every area of my life and requires a constant focus.

Slide #3

- You have a desire to give but have nothing to give – Money Problem
- You have a desire to give but have tied up your resources and can't give – Management Problem
- You have no desire to give, no desire for biblical management for any part of your life – Heart Problem

Slide #4

Biblical money management is the result of life management required of those who know Christ as savior and Lord.

Slide #5

- **Acts 2:36** Therefore let all the house of Israel know assuredly that God has made this Jesus, whom you crucified, both Lord and Christ.
- **Acts 16:31** So they said, "Believe on the Lord Jesus Christ, and you will be saved, you and your household."
- **Romans 10:9** That if you confess with your mouth the Lord Jesus and believe in your heart that God has raised Him from the dead, you will be saved.

Slide #6

A Call to Salvation is a call to...

accept Jesus as Savior,
submit to Him as your Lord,
become a disciple: a disciplined follower of the Lord Jesus Christ.

Slide #7

Purpose of the Series
- Encourage every person toward a biblical perspective on managing their money properly and wisely.
- Expose money problems as indicators that spiritual and biblical principles are being violated
- Encourage honest evaluation of life habits and change the way we think about and use money
- Encourage every person to fast and pray about being a good steward
- Encourage a liberal spirit of giving with a spirit of faith and expectation
- Encourage parents to teach their children through example and instruction how to live according to biblical values and priorities

Slide #8

Biblical Money Management Principles
- God has given us our life, health, talents and allowed us to work and receive money and possessions.
- God desires to bless us but requires us to manage wisely what we already have.
- God can bring prosperity into our life, give us more than enough and allow us to receive abundance of money, knowing we have learned the purpose of prosperity.

Slide #9

The World of a Biblical Steward

STEWARDSHIP: The careful and responsible management of that which God has entrusted to our care: our time, strength, talents and money

GIVING: Giving activates divine law that releases blessings of God in our personal world (Pr 3:9-10)

RECEIVING: God responds to our giving by opening up opportunities to receive divine provisions both directly and indirectly from His hand (Mal 3:9-10)

MANAGING: God expects and requires believers to biblically manage their life, including their money (2 Tim 2:7; Pr 16:32; Josh 1:8; Ps 1:1-3)

PROSPERING: God desires that we receive abundantly and have more than enough so as to become a liberal giver (1 Chr 4:10; Pr 3:6)

Empowering The Giving Of Your Church
We Can Touch The World

WE CAN TOUCH THE WORLD

SERMON #4

We Can Touch The World
Building Bridges to Reach Local, National and International People to Receive Christ and Biblical Resources

A church for every people and the gospel for every person
John 4:34 "Jesus said to them, "My food is to do the will of Him who sent Me, and to finish His work.""
(Revelation 7:9-10; Proverbs 29:18; Acts 1:8; Matthew 28:19-20)

INTRODUCTION This message is not an attempt to help you focus on your own problems, struggles, finances, etc. If a house is on fire with children inside, why should it concern me if my nails are not filed and polished, my clothes are not designer or a house only has 1½ bathrooms! The multitude of Revelation 7:9-10 is the goal and the focus. We must keep our eyes on the true gold, the true purpose for living.

Facts About the World

a. 1.6 billion never heard the gospel, 27% of the world's population[1]

b. 16,000 languages have no scripture, no native pastor or church to attend

c. 95% of the world's pastors live in 5% of the world population. Only 9% of the world speaks English and 96% of the churches income is spent among the 9%. There are 37,000 Protestant missionaries from the US and Canada and all over the world. They come from 620 Protestant agencies working in 182 countries.

d. There are 2 billion Christians (33% of the world's population), 1.2 billion Muslims, 811 million Hindus and 360 million Buddhists.[2]

Facts About the USA

a. 35 million Hispanics in the US, 20 million of those are under 30 years of age[3]

b. 10 million Asians[4]

c. Ethnic groups are now 36% of the total population.[5]
   - The second largest Cuban city in the world is Miami.
   - The second largest Mexican city in the world is Los Angeles
   - The second largest Filipino city in the world is Los Angeles.
   - The second largest Korean city in the world is Los Angeles.
   - The second largest Samoan city in the world is Los Angeles. In fact, there are more Samoans living in the US than there are living in Samoa.
   - The second largest Polish city is Chicago

d. Citizens of 200 countries attend our universities. International students are now 450,000. 45 past foreign presidents attended US universities.

e. 6-7 million Muslims in the US and about 1,200 mosques. Experts say Islam could become the second-largest religion in the nation within a matter of decades.[6] There are 10,000 Muslims and 6 mosques in Portland!

f. 2.4 million Hindus in the US

g. For the first time in history, representatives from every nation on earth live in one place—America.

God is a World Person

Oswald J. Smith: His church in Toronto, Canada has contributed 23 million do missions since 1928. He says, "The supreme task of the church is the evangelization of the world. When God loved, He loved a world. When He gave His Son, He gave His Son for a world. When Jesus Christ died, He died for a world. God's vision is a world vision. That is the vision He wants us to have."

- JOHN 3:16 For God so loved the *world* that He gave His only begotten Son, that whoever believes in Him should not perish but have everlasting life.
- JOHN 1:29 The next day John saw Jesus coming toward him, and said, "Behold! The Lamb of God who takes away the sin of the *world*!"
- 2 CORINTHIANS 5:19 That is, that God was in Christ reconciling the *world* to Himself, not imputing their trespasses to them, and has committed to us the word of reconciliation.
- MATTHEW 24:14 And this gospel of the kingdom will be preached in all the *world* as a witness to all the nations, and then the end will come.

World Christian Attitude: Links my small circle of activity to the global community. It reminds me that my Christian faith rises above cultures; it knows neither national boundaries nor ethnic limitations.

I. OUR VISION

    A.   Our CBC Vision Statement
(Ephesians 3:20; Genesis 49:22)

EXALTING THE LORD
by dynamic, Holy Spirit inspired worship, praise and prayer. Giving our time, talents and gifts as an offering to the Lord.

EQUIPPING THE CHURCH
to fulfill her destiny through godly vision, biblical teaching and pastoral ministries, bringing believers to maturity in Christ and effective ministry, resulting in a restored triumphant church.

EXTENDING THE KINGDOM
of God through the church, to our city, our nation and the world through aggressive evangelism, training leaders, planting churches and sending missionaries and mission teams.

B. Our vision is to be:

1. **An international, multi-cultural church.** We have always desired to reach the nations of the world, but we are learning that the nations are literally here at our door. We want to build a bridge of love and trust to the people groups of our city. The central part of our strategy is to target different areas and people, reach out and build relationships, gather them in ethnic fellowships, and welcome them into the family as one church. *"... no longer foreigners and aliens, but fellow citizens with God's people and members of God's household"*

   a. Ethnic groups:
   1) Asian   4) Indonesia   6) Romanian
   2) Burmese   5) Japanese   7) Russian/Ukranian
   3) Hispanic   6) Laotian   8) Sudanese

   b. ESL, Literacy program, interpretation of services into five of nine languages

2. **A world vision church.** *"Therefore go and make disciples of all nations...baptizing...teaching them to obey everything I have commanded..."* There are 239 nations and 350 large world-cities that need apostolic churches. We need a world faith for a world vision! We by ourselves can't do this, but we can partner with the Body of Christ, mark our cities and do our share.

3. **A bridge building church.** There is no doubt that you have seen a bridge and it is equally likely that you have traveled over one. In fact, most of us have constructed a bridge. Who hasn't laid a plank or log down over a small stream to cross without getting their feet wet? A bridge provides passage over some type of obstacle: a river, a valley, a road or a set of railroad tracks. The type of bridge used depends on various features of the obstacle. The main feature that controls the type of bridge is the size of the obstacle.
   a. *The City*: city pastor meetings, Stitches, community service
   b. *The Nation*: church planting, equipping pastors, Washington DC prayer house
   c. *The Nations*: missionaries and Bible colleges/training centers

4. **A Great Commission church**; this vision is vital to any healthy local church. From the outset it provides a sense of purpose and direction for the people of God. The Holy Spirit desires that we learn to think globally and eternally.
   (Acts 1:8)

II. TOUCHING THE WORLD NECESSITATES BEING TOUCHED FIRST
(Isaiah 6:6-7)

A. Touching the world begins by God touching you.
1. CBC Member Profile: "The goal of our ministry to every member is to help them become a person who is born again, water baptized and filled with the Spirit, who is faithful to the corporate church gathering, cell ministry and School of Equipping; joyfully gives their tithes and offerings, enjoys prayer and worship, has a heart for winning our city to Christ and a vision for world missions, upholds family values and loves God with all their heart, soul, mind and strength.
2. God desires to touch your heart.

B. Touching the world begins by you touching God

1. When you reach out to God and touch His fire, His burden for the lost, you will change.

2. When you touch God, you touch His love, passion and compassion.

C. Touching the world begins by you touching people today

1. The Coles touched Laotians here in Portland first and began a ministry to them here before they went to the nations of the world.

2. The way to become a world-touching person is to begin with first steps: people and giving.

III. OUR RESPONSE

- C.T. Studd, famous Cambridge rugby player and missionary to China: "If Christ be Lord and he died for me, then no sacrifice can be to great for me to make for Him."
- Winston Churchill: "Give us the tools and we'll finish the job."

A. Touching Our World: A Personal Response

1. Sacrifice: <u>Buy the Field</u>
(Matthew 13:44)

   a. Field = The harvest of souls the world over
   b. Treasure = The work of God and of the Holy Spirit within the field. The treasure is the people.

		c.	Commitment = Sell all he has; total commitment to that vision. Possess the field; possess the treasure. Must make it a priority commitment.
		d.	Simplicity has to do with reorganizing your priorities of time and money to make room for missions.

	2.	<u>Equal Reward</u>
		(1 Samuel 30:24)

B.	Touching Our World: A Corporate Response
	(Luke 12:48; Psalm 2:8)

	1.	A commitment to becoming a Great Commission church

	2.	A commitment to developing Holy Spirit-inspired strategies to reach our world

	3.	A commitment to intercessory prayer for "all nations" of the world

	4.	A commitment to sacrificial giving of our best leaders to missions work

	5.	A commitment to sacrificial giving of our money, now, today for missions
		(Matthew 6:19-21)

	6.	Planned Giving

		a.	Missions giving is one way to reach out. If you can't go, send someone else. We must get the job done.

		b.	John Wesley: Through sacrifice he helped others. He lived a simple life but gave over $500,000 to missions. "Gladly would I again make the floor my bed, a box my chair, a box my table, rather than that men should perish for want of the knowledge of the savior."

		c.	The personal income of all church members in the US is 15, 198 billion per year. The income of global foreign missions is 15 billion.[7]
			• We spend $600 on luxuries for every $1.00 to missions.

		d.	Each family, each person to give a minimum of $15.00 toward missions. Some may be challenged to give more. Our mission goal this year is $300,000. This will be accomplished by our Mission Faith Pledge. A commitment made will be for one year at a time.

During the Second World War, Winston Churchill, then prime minister of Great Britain, set out to 'win with words' over Hitler by raising the morale of the nation. Not only did he visit troops and factories, but he went to the out-of-the-way coal-mining towns. On one visit to the hard-working coal miners, the prime minister urged them to see their significance in the total effort for victory. He told them:

"We will be victorious! We will preserve our freedom. And years from now when our freedom is secure and peace reigns, your children and children's children will come and they will say to you, 'What did you do to win our freedom in that great war?' And one will say, 'I marched with the Eighth Army!' Someone else will proudly say, 'I manned a submarine.' And another will say, 'I guided the ships that moved the troops and supplies.' And still another will say, 'I doctored the wounds!'"
Then the great statesman paused. The dirty-faced miners sat in silence and awe, waiting for him to proceed.

"They will come to you," he shouted, "and you will say, with equal right and equal pride, 'I cut the coal! I cut the coal that fueled the ships that moved the supplies! That's what I did. I cut the coal!'" (A Force in the Earth, page 164)

---

[1] Status of Global Mission, 2001, in Context of 20th and 21st Centuries, January 2001.
[2] Status of Global Mission, 2001, in Context of 20th and 21st Centuries, January 2001.
[3] U.S. Census Bureau, Census 2000, unpublished tables (Table 9; March 20, 2001).
[4] U.S. Census Bureau, Census 2000, unpublished tables (Table 1; April 2, 2001).
[5] Gerry Johnson. *Preparing the Congregation for Ethnic Ministry* (paper presented in Portland, Oregon, November 18, 1998).
[6] Gustav Niebuhr. *US Muslim Population Flourishing* Oregonian ()
[7] Status of Global Mission, 2001, in Context of 20th and 21st Centuries, January 2001.

Slide #1

Slide #2
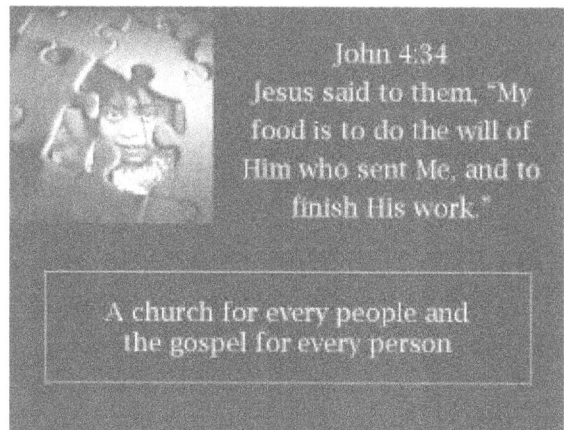

Slide #3
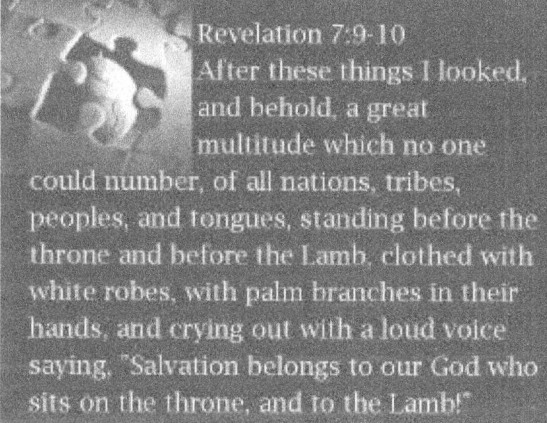

Slide #4
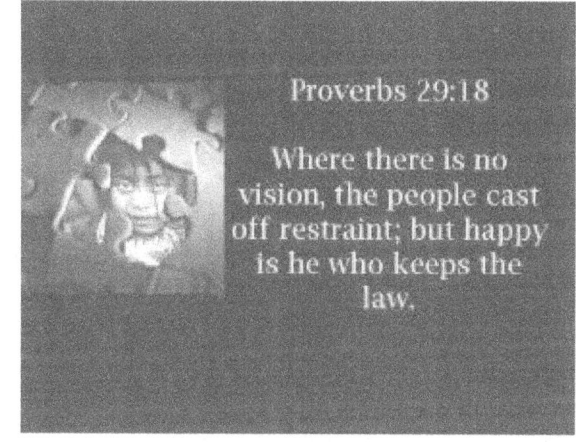

Slide #5
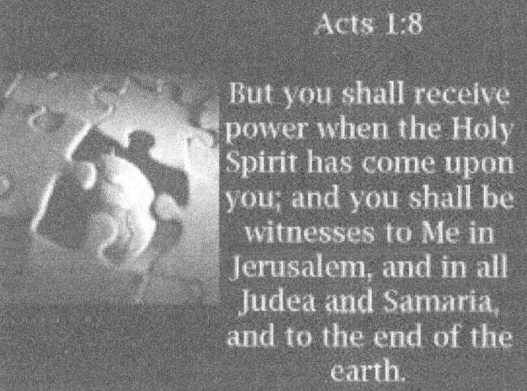

Slide #6
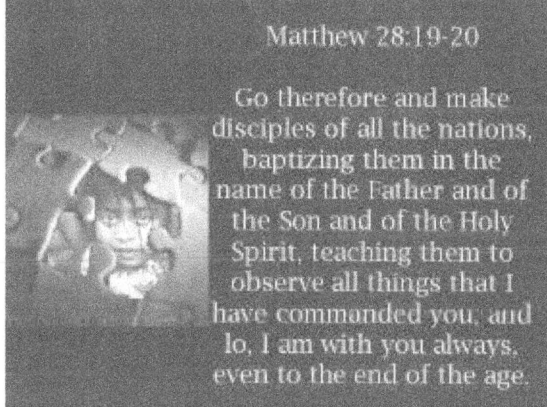

Slide #7

City Bible Church
Vision Statement

Exalting the Lord
Equipping the Saints
Extending the Kingdom

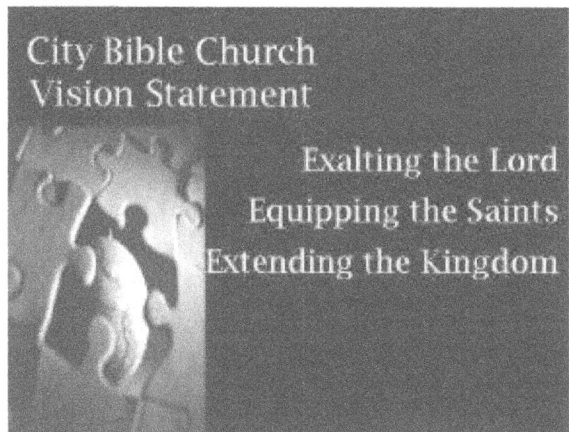

Slide #8

Our Vision Is To Be...

An international, multi-cultural church
A world vision church
A bridge building church
A Great Commission Church

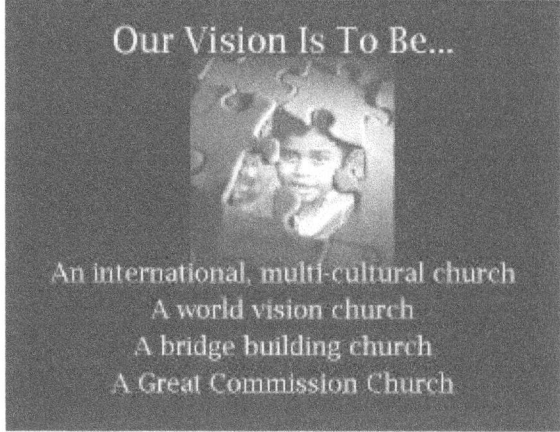

Slide #9

Touching the World Necessitates Being Touched First

Touching the world begins with:
- God touching you
- You touching God
- You touching people today

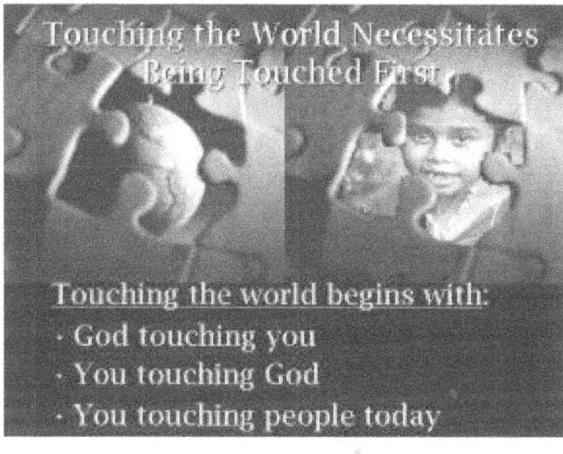

Slide #10

Our Corporate Response Is To Make a Commitment To:

1. Become a Great Commission church.
2. Develop Holy Spirit-inspired strategies to reach our world.
3. Intercessory prayer for "all nations" of the world
4. Sacrificial giving of our best leaders to missions work
5. Sacrificial giving of our money now, today, for missions

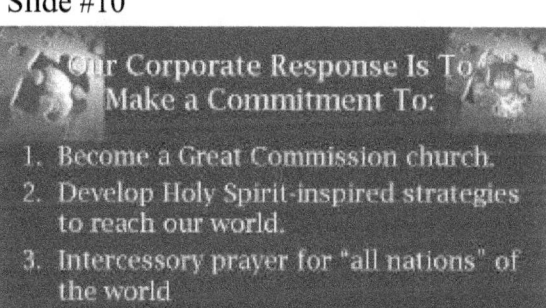

Empowering The Giving Of Your Church
The Call to Great Faith

THE CALL TO GREAT FAITH

SERMON #5

The Call to Great Faith
The Biblical Responsibility of Every Believer

(Ephesians 3:20; Luke 7:9; Hebrews 11:6; Romans 10:17)

"Some say that faith is the gift of God. So is the air but you have to breathe it; so is bread but you have to eat it; so is water but you have to drink it. Some are wanting some miraculous kind of feeling. That is not faith. "Faith comes by hearing and hearing by the Word of God (Romans 10:17)." That is whence faith comes. It is not for me to sit down and wait for faith to come stealing over me with a strong sensation; but it is for me to take God at His word." (D.L. Moody)

Great Faith:
- Great faith sees the invisible, believes the incredible and receives the impossible.
- Great faith sees the promised blessings as if they were present possessions.
- Great faith believes God to be a good God, a God of abundance, an "all things are possible" God.
- Great faith believes God is all-powerful, at all times, in every circumstance. He is a God who is able to do anything.
- Great faith believes God desires to bless His people with great provisions financially and spiritually.

INTRODUCTION: Faith is a basic foundation of the Christian life, without which it is impossible to please God or to receive anything from Him (Hebrews 11:6). A life of faith is essential because everything in our spiritual life stems from faith. The scripture exhorts us in II Peter 1:5 to "add to our faith." Faith is the first step. Ephesians 2:8 "For by grace are you saved through faith… It is the gift of God." Faith is not a product of our emotions, our thinking or our will. Faith comes from God and God alone. It can be developed. Faith is the means by which we live our whole Christian life. Galatians 2:20 says, "I live by the faith of the Son of God." Faith is not something we simply receive once. It is something that must be ever increasing in our lives. The Lord wants to enlarge and expand our capacity to receive more of His life transforming faith. We must remove the hindrances to the growth and development of faith: wrong concepts and ideas about faith; hardness of heart and rebellion; cares, riches and pleasures of this life; unbelief; our intellectual and natural mind; doubt, etc.

Luke 17:5 And the apostles said to the Lord, "Increase our faith."
2 Cor 4:13 And since we have the same spirit of faith, according to what is written, "I believed and therefore I spoke," we also believe and therefore speak,
Matt 9:28 And when He had come into the house, the blind men came to Him. And Jesus said to them, "Do you believe that I am able to do this?" They said to Him, "Yes, Lord."

I. FAITH DEFINED
(Hebrews 11:1-2)

A. Faith is that substance, confidence, substructure of things hoped for
- Faith enables us to treat things hoped for as a property of which we hold the deed

1. Substance – hupostasis – "reality which gives a firm guarantee"
   a. Used five times in scripture: 2 Cor. 9:4, 11:17; Heb. 1:3, 3:14, 11:1
   b. Definition
      - "Underlying realty behind something"
      - "Substructure that which stands under"
      - "that which underlies"
      - "Proof of things one cannot see"
      - "Something that underlies visible conditions and guarantees a future possessions"

2. This would mean that things that have no reality in themselves are made real, given substance by faith. There are realities for which we have no material evidence though they are not the less real for that faith enables us to know that they exist and while we have no certainty apart from faith does give us genuine certainty.

3. Faith prays believing that you have already received them
(Mark 11:24)
   - Faith sees the invisible, believes the incredible and receives the impossible!
   - Hudson Taylor: On the way to China, ship was caught in a calm, no wind, drifting around cannibal Island, captain ask Taylor to pray, Taylor said, I will pray provided you set your sail to catch the breeze! I will not pray unless you prepare for the answer.

B. Faith is the conviction of thing not seen
Hebrews 11:2 "....seeing Him who is invisible..."
- Amplified: "...being the proof of things we do not see and the conviction of them reality...<u>faith perceiving as real fact what is not revealed to the senses</u>"
- New English Bible: "...and makes us certain of realities we do <u>not see</u>"

1. Conviction – Elenkos = "a proof or test," may be used as a legal term with a meaning like cross-examining.
2. Faith is the basis of all that we hope for, is that by which we test things unseen. We have no material way often assessing the significance of the immaterial, but Christians have faith and by thins they test all things.
3. Faith is the demonstration of things not seen.

II. Faith In A Great God
(Titus 2:13)

- In this verse, the Greek word for great is *megas*. We live in a day of mega-trends, mega-bytes, mega-deals, but also a mega-God!

A. Definitions from "Random House Unabridged Dictionary, 2nd Edition

    1. **Great**
        a. Unusually or comparatively large in size or dimension.
        b. Unusual or considerable in degree, power, intensity.
        c. Wonderful; first-rate; very good.
        d. Notable; remarkable; exceptionally outstanding.
        e. Of noble or lofty character.
        f. Chief or principal,
        g. Of extraordinary power; having unusual merit; very admirable
        h. Those holding positions of authority

    2. **Awesome**
        a. Inspiring awe
        b. Showing or characterized by awe

    3. **Awe**
- an overwhelming feeling or reverence, admiration, fear, etc., produced by that which is grand, sublime, extremely powerful, or the like.

B. Great and Awesome God in Scripture
- God is a good God, a God of abundance, healing and miracles. He is a God who does great things, a big God, a living God, a great God. All things are possible with God. There are no limitations. Nothing discourages God.

    1. Old Testament
Dt 7:21 You shall not be terrified of them; for the LORD your God, the **great and awesome God**, *is* among you.
Dt 10:17 For the LORD your God *is* God of gods and Lord of lords, the **great God, mighty and awesome**, who shows no partiality nor takes a bribe.
Neh 1:5 And I said: "I pray, LORD God of heaven, O great and **awesome God**, *You* who keep *Your* covenant and mercy with those who love You and observe Your commandments."
Ne 4:14 And I looked, and arose and said to the nobles, to the leaders, and to the rest of the people, "Do not be afraid of them. Remember the Lord, **great and awesome**, and fight for your brethren, your sons, your daughters, your wives, and your houses.
Ne 9:32 Now therefore, our God, The **great, the mighty, and awesome** God, Who keeps covenant and mercy: Do not let all the trouble seem small

before You That has come upon us, Our kings and our princes, Our priests and our prophets, Our fathers and on all Your people, from the days of the kings of Assyria until this day.

Da 9:4 And I prayed to the LORD my God, and made confession, and said, "O Lord, great and **awesome God**, who keeps His covenant and mercy with those who love Him, and with those who keep His commandments,

1 Chronicles 17:21 And who *is* like Your people Israel, the one nation on the earth whom God went to redeem for Himself *as* a people--**to make for Yourself a name by great and awesome deeds**, by driving out nations from before Your people whom You redeemed from Egypt?

2. In the New Testament

Luke 1:32 He will be **great**, and will be called the Son of the Highest; and the Lord God will give Him the throne of His father David.

Heb 13:20 Now may the God of peace who brought up our Lord Jesus from the dead, that **great Shepherd of the sheep**, through the blood of the everlasting covenant

Rev 15:3 They sing the song of Moses, the servant of God, and the song of the Lamb, saying: "**Great and marvelous are Your works**, lord God Almighty! Just and true are Your ways, O King of the saints!

Rev 19:17 Then I saw an angel standing in the sun; and he cried with a loud voice, saying to all the birds that fly in the midst of heaven, "Come and gather together for the supper of the **great God**,

III. FAITH IN A GREAT VISION WITH A GREAT FUTURE

- A vision-less church is an impoverished church.
- Dream big, pray big, ask big, minister big.
- No dream, no vision, no need, no ministry transcends the capacity of our God.
- Great leaders see the future first!
- In spite of secularism and modernism, God is the future. The gospel works for all ages.
- "Give up your small ambitions. Come save the world." (Saint Francis)
- "The most pathetic person in the world is one who has sight but has no vision." (Helen Keller)

(Isaiah 54:2; Jeremiah 29:11; Ephesians 1:18)

Prov 29:18 Where there is no revelation, the people cast off restraint; but happy is he who keeps the law.
- *Where there is no vision, the people perish (KJV).*
- Where there is no vision (revelation), the people are unrestrained (NASB).
- Where there is no progressive vision, the people dwell carelessly (Swedish).

A. The Working Definition of Vision

Vision is that which a congregation perceives by the Holy Spirit as pertaining to God's purpose for them, thereby creating spiritual momentum resulting in spiritual advancement and maintained through spiritual warfare.

Vision is…
1. Having a view from above
2. The ability of seeing into the future, having foresight into something that is attainable by a person or a group.
3. An informed bridge from the present to the future
4. A clear mental image of a preferable future imparted by God through His chosen servants and is based upon an accurate understanding of God, self and circumstances (Barna).

B. The Seven Nevers of Vision

1. Never allow the world, the flesh or the devil to shape your vision, for vision shapes destiny.

2. Never allow smallness of vision to rule your life.
(1 Chronicles 4:9-10)

3. Never allow those who have no faith to influence you.
(Hebrews 11:1)
- Strained faith, defective faith, wounded faith, faulty faith, dead faith. We need LIVING faith.
- No faith people always doubt new or big ideas and have many reasons why something won't work.
- In 1840 they believed anyone traveling at 30 mph would suffocate.
- In 1878 they believed electric lights were unworthy of serious attention.
- In 1901 they believed that men would never fly.
- In 1926 the idea of traveling to the moon was preposterous.
- ❖ "The man who says it cannot be done should not interrupt the man doing it." (Chinese proverb)

4. Never allow discouragement to dominate your faith in God fulfilling your vision.
- Whatever it is, however impossible it seems, whatever the obstacle that lies between you and it, if it is noble, if it is consistent with God's kingdom, you must hunger after it and stretch yourself to reach it.

5. Never allow circumstances to limit your vision; change your circumstances through faith.
    (Isaiah 50:11)
    - "There are a lot of ways to become a failure, but never taking a chance is the most successful."

6. Never allow finances to become the dictator to the vision. God is your resource.
    - Walt Disney never worried about the finances because he was excited about his vision.
    - People will give toward a great vision. Resources will follow!
    - This must be done with wisdom.

7. Never allow failure to set your course in life. Get up again, try again, never give up!
    (Micah 7:7-8)
    - ❖ "Never give up for that is just the place and time that the tide will turn." (Harriet Beecher Stowe)

IV. FAITH FOR A GREAT HARVEST OF LOST PEOPLE

(John 6:2-3)

A. Principle/Prophetic: lifting eyes, seeing, multitude coming
   (John 6:5; Acts 16:5)

B. Faith to Reach Multitudes
   Psalm 42:4 When I remember these things, I pour out my soul within me. For I used to go with the *multitude*; I went with them to the house of God, with the voice of joy and praise, with a multitude that kept a pilgrim feast.
   Revelation 7:9 After these things I looked, and behold, a *great multitude* which no one could number, of all nations, tribes, peoples, and tongues, standing before the throne and before the Lamb, clothed with white robes, with palm branches in their hands,
   Revelation 19:1 After these things I heard a loud voice of a *great multitude* in heaven, saying, Alleluia! Salvation and glory and honor and power belong to the Lord our God!
   Revelation 19:6 I heard, as it were, the voice of a *great multitude*, as the sound of many waters and as the sound of mighty thunderings, saying, Alleluia! For the Lord God Omnipotent reigns!
   Mark 6:34 Jesus, when He came out, saw a *great multitude* and was moved with compassion for them because they were like sheep not having a shepherd. So he began to teach them many things
   Mark 2:13 He went out again by the sea; and all the *multitude* came to Him, and He taught them.

Acts 4:32 Now the ***multitude*** of those who believed were of one heart and one soul; neither did anyone say that any of the things he possessed was his own, but they had all things in common.

Acts 6:5 And the saying pleased the whole ***multitude***. And they chose Stephen, a man full of faith and the Holy Spirit, and Philip, Prochorus, Nicanor, Timon, Parmenas, and Nicolas, a proselyte from Antioch,

Acts 14:1 Now it happened in Iconium that they went together to the synagogue of the Jews, and so spoke that a ***great multitude*** both of the Jews and of the Greeks believed.

Acts 17:4 And some of them were persuaded; and a ***great multitude*** of the devout Greeks, and not a few of the leading women, joined Paul and Silas.

V. FAITH FOR A GOD OF GREAT PROVISION

A. A God who is able
(Ephesians 3:20)

That is able to do **exceeding abundantly:** It is impossible to express the full meaning of these words, God is omnipotent, therefore he is able to do all things, and able to do huper, ek, perissou – superabundantly above the greatest abundance. And who can doubt this, who has any rational or Scriptural views of his power or his love! (from Adam Clarke Commentary)

1. Exceedingly: Extreme, extraordinary, surpass, to go beyond the limits of, more than.

2. Abundantly: To be overabundant, enough and much to spare, occurring in a marked abundance, plentiful, superabundant in quantity or superior in quality, more than is necessary, increase, extraordinary, unusual, strange, overflowing, surplus.

B. Great Provision Scriptures
   ❖ "You have never tested God's resources until you have attempted the impossible!"
   1. Luke 6:38 Give, and it will be given to you: good measure, pressed down, shaken together, and running over will be put into your bosom. For with the same measure that you use, it will be measured back to you.
   2. Deut 8:13 And when your herds and your flocks multiply, and your silver and your gold are multiplied, and all that you have is multiplied;
   3. Deut 8:18 And you shall remember the Lord your God, for it is He who gives you power to get wealth, that He may establish His covenant which He swore to your fathers, as it is this day.
   4. Phil 4:19 And my God shall supply all your need according to His riches in glory by Christ Jesus.
   5. Ps 118:25 Save now, I pray, O Lord; O Lord, I pray, send now prosperity.

6. 3 Jn 1:2 Beloved, I pray that you may prosper in all things and be in health, just as your soul prospers.
7. Prov 10:22 The blessing of the Lord makes one rich, and He adds no sorrow with it.
8. Luke 15:17 But when he came to himself, he said, 'How many of my father's hired servants have bread enough and to spare, and I perish with hunger!
9. Phil 4:18 Indeed I have all and abound. I am full, having received from Epaphroditus the things sent from you, a sweet-smelling aroma, an acceptable sacrifice, well pleasing to God.
10. 2 Cor 8:2 That in a great trial of affliction the abundance of their joy and their deep poverty abounded in the riches of their liberality.
11. John 10:10 The thief does not come except to steal, and to kill, and to destroy. I have come that they may have life, and that they may have it more abundantly.
12. Matt 7:11 If you then, being evil, know how to give good gifts to your children, how much more will your Father who is in heaven give good things to those who ask Him!
13. Matt 13:12 For whoever has, to him more will be given, and he will have abundance; but whoever does not have, even what he has will be taken away from him.

Slide #1

Slide #2
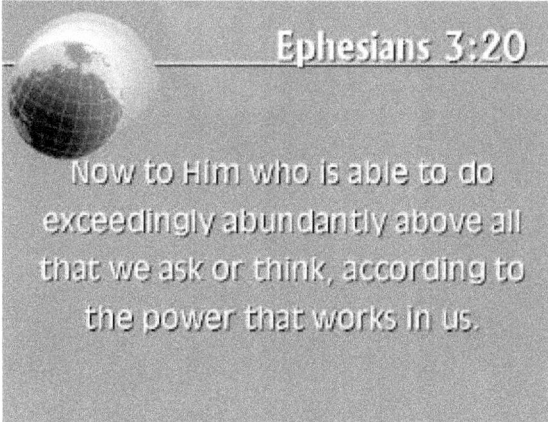

Slide #3
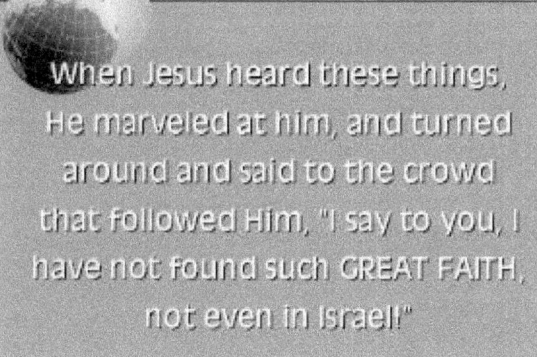

Slide #4
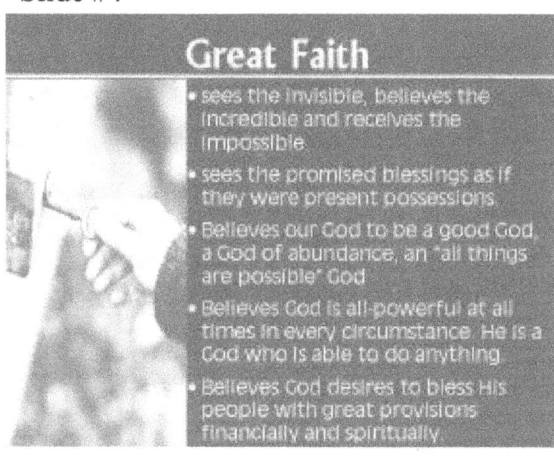

Slide #5
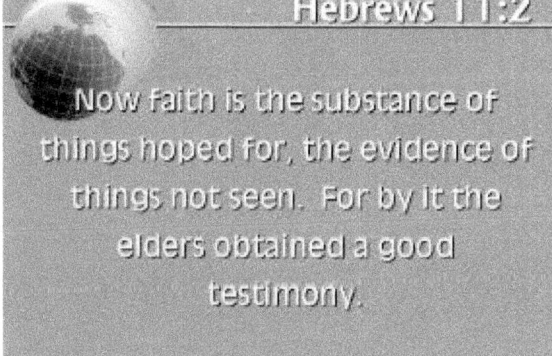

Slide #6
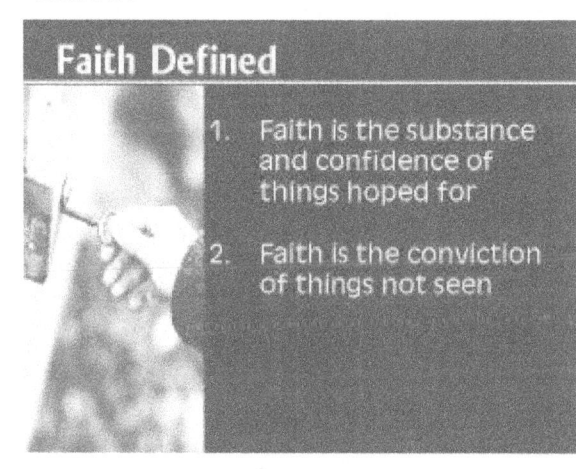

Slide #7

Faith in a Great God

Titus 2:13 Looking for the blessed hope and glorious appearing of our great God and Savior Jesus Christ,

Dt 10:17 For the Lord your God is God of gods and Lord of lords, the great God, mighty and awesome...

Slide #8

Faith in a Great Vision with a Great Future

Vision is that which a congregation perceives by the Holy Spirit as pertaining to God's purpose for them, thereby creating spiritual momentum resulting in spiritual advancement and maintained through spiritual warfare.

Slide #9

Seven Nevers of Vision

1. Never allow the world, flesh or the devil to shape your vision for vision shapes destiny.
2. Never allow smallness of vision to rule your life.
3. Never allow those who have no faith to influence you.
4. Never allow discouragement to dominate your faith in God fulfilling your vision.
5. Never allow circumstances to limit your vision.
6. Never allow finances to become the dictator to the vision. God is your resource.
7. Never allow failure to set your course in life.

Slide #10

Faith for a Great Harvest of Lost People

John 6:2-3
Acts 16:5
Psalm 42:4
Psalm 109:30
Revelation 7:9
Revelation 19:6

Slide #11

Faith for a God of Great Provision

A God Who Is Able

Now to Him who is able to do exceedingly abundantly above all that we ask or think, according to the power that works in us

(Ephesians 3:20)

# Empowering The Giving Of Your Church
Great Vision Takes the Challenge

GREAT VISION TAKES THE CHALLENGE

SERMON #6

Great Vision Takes the Challenge

1 Chronicles 4:10; Joshua 17:17-18; Numbers 14:24

- President Woodrow Wilson (28th president): "We grow great by dreams. All big men and women are dreamers."[1]
- A ship in port is safe, but this is not what ships are built for.
- The problem is usually not what you can't do. It is what you won't do!

Great vision is:
- A vision that is as big as God.
- A vision that is as big as the scriptures.
- A vision that is as big as our faith to believe and receive.

INTRODUCTION:
The book of Joshua is divided into three parts: (1) entering the land, Joshua 1-5; (2) overcoming the land, Joshua 6-12; and (3) occupying the land, Joshua 13-24. Joshua's central theme is the victory of faith. The book of Numbers was the failure of unbelief, failure to enter, failure to overcome, failure to occupy. We are challenged to live with a great vision that demands great faith, a faith that reaches forward, a faith that stretches into the new. Faith lives on challenges. Faith rises to meet the enemies of God. Faith never stands still. It possesses. It moves ahead.

I. A GREAT PEOPLE WHO WILL NOT BE RESTRICTED

(Josh 17:14-18)

    A. Definitions: "too confined is not enough." Restricted: curbed, limited, restrained, confined, cramped, small

        1. Those who shrink to the size of their environment like a shark in a fish tank grows only to the size of the tank.

        2. Hudson Taylor: "Satan may build a hedge about us and fence us in and hinder our movements, but he cannot roof us in and prevent our looking up!"

        3. Not restricted by life's circumstances that are challenging.

B. Ephraim and Manasseh: Children of Joseph who had dreams and visions in their blood stream.
- Businessman: A highly successful businessman was asked, "How have you done so much in your lifetime?" He replied, "I have dreamed. I have turned my mind loose to imagine what I wanted to do. Then I have gone to bed and thought about my dreams. In the night I dreamt about my dreams. And when I awoke in the morning, I saw the way to make my dreams real. While other people were saying, 'You can't do that, it isn't possible,' I was well on my way to achieving what I wanted."[2]

1. Joseph: To add increase.
   a. God desires to add and bring increase to your soul, to your ministry, to your life, to our church.
   b. Each of us may be sure that if God sends us over rocky paths, he will provide us with sturdy shoes.

2. Joseph: Here comes the dreamer

3. Joseph: From the pit to Potiphar's house, prison and then ruler, a great vision with a great price to pay

II. A PEOPLE WHO WILL NOT BE SATISFIED WITH A SMALL VISION

(Joshua 17:17)

> If you are a great people, be it so.
> But if you are a great people,
> You must be capable of great deeds.
> So get on with it!

A. There are great opportunities before you, wooded areas that no one has cleared because the work was hard and dangerous

B. There are great rewards lying within reach but you must direct your energies to them.

C. There are great enemies who possess your lot of inheritance. Go up and take what is yours.

D. There is no room for blaming God as to our one lot in life, our one talent, our limited life. We are to not complain about what has been dealt us but to change it by work, vision and warfare.

- In ancient times, a king placed a boulder in the middle of the road, then hid to see if anyone would remove it. Some of the king's wealthiest merchants and courtiers simply walked around it. Many loudly blamed the king for not keeping the roads clear, but none did anything about getting the big stone out of the way. Then a peasant came along carrying a load of vegetables. On approaching the boulder, the peasant laid down his burden and tried to move the stone to the side of the road. After much pushing and straining, he finally succeeded. As the peasant picked up his load of vegetables, he noticed a purse lying in the road where the boulder had been. The purse contained many gold coins and a note from the king indicating that the gold was for the person who removed the boulder from the roadway. The peasant learned what many others never understand. Every obstacle presents an opportunity to improve one's condition.
- Ten year old, Sarah, was born with a muscle missing in her foot and wore a brace all the time. She came home one day to tell her father me she had competed in "field day", where they have lots of races and other competitive events. "Daddy, I won two of the races!" Her father was amazed, winning two races with a brace on! Then Sarah said, "I had an advantage." Of course, her dad thought, she must have been given a headstart to have been able to win. But before her father could say anything, she said, "<u>Daddy, I didn't get a head start... My advantage was I had to try harder!</u>"

III. A Great People Who Have the Courage to Possess The Vision

Walt Disney: "Several years ago I met a gentleman who served on one of Walt Disney's original advisory boards. What amazing stories he told! Those early days were tough; but that remarkable, creative visionary refused to give up. I especially appreciated the man's sharing with me how Disney responded to disagreement. He said that Walt would occasionally present some unbelievable, extensive dream he was entertaining. Almost without exception, the members of his board would gulp, blink, and stare back at him in disbelief, resisting even the thought of such a thing. But unless every member resisted the idea, Disney usually didn't pursue it. Yes, you read that correctly. The challenge wasn't big enough to merit his time and creative energy unless they were unanimously in disagreement!"[3]

A. **Go up:** Do not stay within your set boundaries. Do not blame God or circumstances. Move out. Get up and go up. See the vision set before you, before you, before us, and make a decision to go up to meet the challenges.
(Josh 17:15; Gen 35:1; ; Num 13:30; Deut 9:23; Josh 1:9)

B. **Cut down:** Remove all obstacles. Clear away the hindrances. Make room for the vision to be enlarged. Clear the ground.
(Josh 17:18; Josh 17:15; Deut 7:5; Deut 12:3)
- Mike Philips: "In the spiritual realm, adversity signifies advance. If there are no problems, no tensions, no uncertainties, things are not functioning according to the biblical norm… The higher you set goals, the greater the pressure you'll experience!"

C. **Drive out:** Any and all enemies must be drive out through faith, prayer, fasting. Enemies that have occupied your land, your vision, your future – drive them out now.
(Josh 17:18)
- Hebrew: to occupy by driving out previous tenants, and possessing in their place; to seize, to inherit; to expel, to dispossess, to take possession off, to inherit, to occupy

1. Canaan land, our vision land, is a land of promise and provision
(Deut 6:10-11)

2. Canaan land, our vision land, is a land of great wealth and riches.
(Ex 3:8; Deut 33:28)

3. Canaan land, our vision land, is a land of warfare and victory over all enemies
(Deut 7:1; 1 John 3:4)
- Our increase and influence is to be through conflict with the enemies of vision and the enemies of increase!

---

[1] www.cyberquotations.com/stories/grow_great_by_dreams.htm
[2] www.cyberquotations.com/stories/grow_great_by_dreams.htm
[3] Charles Swindoll, *Living Above the Level of Mediocrity*, p.107

Slide #1

Great Vision takes the Challenge

Slide #2

Great vision is...

- A vision that is as big as God.
- A vision that is as big as the scriptures.
- A vision that is as big as our faith to believe and receive.

Slide #3

1 Chronicles 4:10

"And Jabez called on the God of Israel saying, 'Oh, that You would bless me indeed, and enlarge my territory, that Your hand would be with me, and that You would keep me from evil, that I may not cause pain!' So God granted him what he requested."

Slide #4

Joshua 17:17-18

"You are a great people and have great power; you shall not have only one lot, but the mountain country shall be yours. Although it is wooded, you shall cut it down, and its farthest extent shall be yours; for you shall drive out the Canaanites, though they have iron chariots and are strong."

Slide #5

Numbers 14:24

"But My servant Caleb, because he has a different spirit in him and has followed Me fully, I will bring into the land where he went, and his descendants shall inherit it."

Slide #6

Joshua 17:14-18

- A great people who will not be restricted
- A great people who will not be satisfied with small vision
- A great people who have the courage to possess the vision.

Slide #1

Great Vision takes the Challenge

Slide #2

Great vision is...

- A vision that is as big as God.
- A vision that is as big as the scriptures.
- A vision that is as big as our faith to believe and receive.

Slide #3

1 Chronicles 4:10

"And Jabez called on the God of Israel saying, 'Oh, that You would bless me indeed, and enlarge my territory, that Your hand would be with me, and that You would keep me from evil, that I may not cause pain!' So God granted him what he requested."

Slide #4

Joshua 17:17-18

"You are a great people and have great power; you shall not have only one lot, but the mountain country shall be yours. Although it is wooded, you shall cut it down, and its farthest extent shall be yours; for you shall drive out the Canaanites, though they have iron chariots and are strong."

Slide #5

Numbers 14:24

"But My servant Caleb, because he has a different spirit in him and has followed Me fully, I will bring into the land where he went, and his descendants shall inherit it."

Slide #6

Joshua 17:14-18

- A great people who will not be restricted
- A great people who will not be satisfied with small vision
- A great people who have the courage to possess the vision.

Slide #7

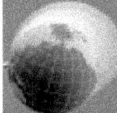
Go up!

Do not stay within your set boundaries.

See the vision before you.

Go up to meet the challenges.

Slide #8

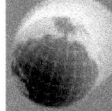
Cut down!

Remove all obstacles.

Clear away hindrances.

Make room for the vision to be enlarged.

Slide #9

Drive out!

Drive out
the enemies through faith, prayer and fasting.

Drive out
the enemies who occupy your land, your vision, your future.

Additional Resources by City Christian Publishing

TO ORDER, CALL: 1.800.777.6057 • www.CityChristianPublishing.com

The Making of a Leader
Biblical Leadership Principles for Today's Leaders
Frank Damazio
ISBN 978-0-914936-84-8

Effective Keys to Successful Leadership
Wisdom and Insight for God's Set Man and the Ministry Leadership Team
Frank Damazio
ISBN 978-0-914936-54-1

The Gate Church
Discover the Authority, Power and Results God Wants for Your Church
Frank Damazio
ISBN 978-1-886849-77-8

Timothy Training Program
Leadership Training for Small Groups and Individuals
Frank Damazio
Teacher
ISBN 978-0-914936-12-1
Student
ISBN 978-0-914936-13-8

52 Offering Prayers & Scriptures
Encouraging the Heart of Giving in the Church
Frank Damazio
ISBN 978-1-59383-047-2

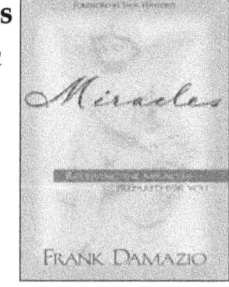

Miracles
Receiving the Miracles Prepared for You
Frank Damazio
ISBN 978-1-886849-83-9

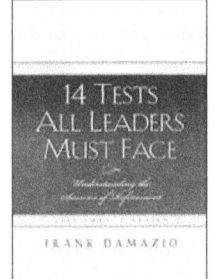

14 Tests All Leaders Must Face
Understanding the Seasons of Refinement
Frank Damazio
ISBN 978-1-59383-057-1

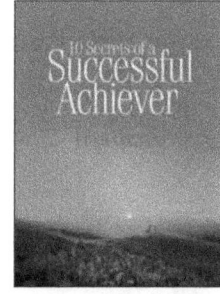

10 Secrets of a Successful Achiever
Living the Life God Intended for You
Frank Damazio
ISBN 978-1-886849-98-3

21 Personal Breakthrough Prayers & Scriptures
Removing Long Standing Obstacles
Frank Damazio
ISBN 978-1-59383-035-9

Empowering Your Preaching
Frank Damazio
Student Handbook
ISBN 978-1-886849-91-4
Audio - 5 CDs
UPC 643101-119426